CAMBRIDGE ASSIGNMENTS IN MUSIC

Instruments of the Orchestra

ROY BENNETT

CAMBRIDGE
UNIVERSITY PRESS

Contents

1
What is an orchestra?

Orchestra is an old Greek word which, rather strangely, really means 'a dancing place'. In Greece, during the 5th century B.C., plays were performed in open-air theatres, called amphitheatres. *Orchestra* was the name given to the space in front of the main acting area which was used by the chorus, who danced as well as sang, and by the instrumentalists.

Much later, at the beginning of the 17th century, in Italy, the first operas were being performed. These were originally intended to be imitations of the ancient Greek dramas, and so the same word *orchestra* was used to describe the space between the stage and the audience occupied by the instrumentalists. But soon *orchestra* came to mean the musicians themselves, and then eventually, the collection of instruments which they played.

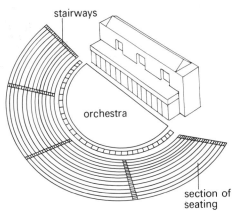

Greek theatre

The orchestra of an early opera house

And so today we use the word *orchestra* to mean a reasonably large collection of instruments playing together as a group. But which instruments exactly? And how many make up 'a reasonably large collection'? The fact is, the number and type of instruments may vary considerably from one piece to another, according to the exact combination which the composer asks for in order to express his musical ideas. Also, the shape and size of the orchestra has been continually changing over the past four centuries. Certain instruments, particularly the brass, have been cleverly developed in ways which make them easier to play – also increasing the number of notes they can play. The range and variety of instrumental tone-colours have gradually increased as new instruments have been invented, then accepted into the orchestra.

Before exploring all these instruments in detail, let us take a look at how an orchestra is arranged on the concert platform.

The sections of the orchestra

Imagine that you are sitting in a concert hall with the orchestra spread out in front of you. This 'reasonably large collection of instruments' is by no means a haphazard grouping of whatever forces happen to be available. It is, in fact, a highly organised and

3

balanced unit made up of four sections or 'families' of instruments:

strings • woodwind • brass • percussion

The instruments in each section share certain 'family likenesses'.
In the string section, sounds are made by causing stretched strings
to vibrate, either by drawing a bow across them, or by plucking
them with the fingers. In the woodwind and brass sections, the
sounds are caused by blowing. Woodwind instruments are mainly made
of wood, and brass instruments may indeed be made of brass, but
there is a more important difference between these two families of
instruments: the way in which the sounds are actually produced.
This will become clearer later on when we look at the instruments
of these two sections in detail. All instruments in the percussion
section are either struck or shaken.

The arrangement of the orchestral sections on the concert platform
is a practical one. Because of their family likenesses, the instruments
of each section are grouped together. The platform is usually
terraced, and the sections are positioned in such a way as to achieve
a balance and blend of the various instrumental sounds and
tone-colours. The conductor must be able to hear each instrument
clearly and of course it is essential that each player should be
able to see the conductor.

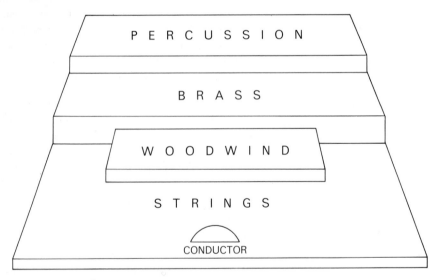

Strings

The strings, who play the most important part in the music, are
placed at the front, spreading right across the platform.
The strings are the 'backbone' of the orchestra - more than half
the members of an orchestra are string players.

The string section consists of:

violins	double basses
violas	harp
cellos	

Woodwind

The woodwind players, who frequently take important solos, sit in the centre of the orchestra – directly facing the conductor, and raised higher than the strings.

The woodwind section includes:

> flutes and piccolo
> oboes and cor anglais
> clarinets and bass clarinet
> bassoons and double bassoon

Brass

The brass instruments are placed behind the woodwind so that their more powerful and weighty tone does not drown the gentler sounds of woodwind and strings. However, being raised higher, they can cut through the texture of the music when necessary with exciting effect.

The brass section includes:

> horns   trombones
> trumpets   tuba

Percussion

Up at the back, on the highest level, is the percussion section, including drums, cymbals, and everything else which can be struck or shaken, crashed or banged. This is sometimes called 'the kitchen department', due to the excessive amount of noise it can make when necessary! Although the percussion section can offer a greater variety of instruments than any other section of the orchestra, these instruments are shared between a few players only.

The main instruments of the percussion section are:

kettle drums	tambourine	castanets
bass drum	glockenspiel	woodblocks
snare drum	xylophone	tam-tam or gong
cymbals	celesta	whip
triangle	tubular bells	maracas

Music to hear

To fix the special sounds of each section of the orchestra in your mind, listen to the beginning of a recording of Benjamin Britten's *The Young Person's Guide to the Orchestra*, which is also known by another title: *Variations on a Theme of Purcell.* Britten begins his piece with six presentations of Purcell's tune:

1 for the full orchestra
2 for the woodwind section only
3 for the brass section
4 for the strings (including harp)
5 for the percussion section, with kettle drums playing the first three notes of the tune
6 for the full orchestra once more

Assignment 1   Listen to the beginning of each of these pieces. In each one, see
if you can identify the section of the orchestra which the composer
chooses to begin the music.

    (a) Mozart: second movement from Symphony No. 39 in E flat major
    (b) Mussorgsky: *Pictures at an Exhibition* (orchestrated by Ravel)
    (c) Debussy: 'Nuages', from *Nocturnes*
    (d) Berlioz: second movement, 'Un Bal', from *Symphonie Fantastique*
    (e) Rossini: Overture to *The Thieving Magpie*
    (f) Tchaikovsky: Fantasy-Overture, *Romeo and Juliet*
    (g) Verdi: 'Grand March', from the opera *Aida*
    (h) Sibelius: third movement from Symphony No. 2 in D major
    (i) Bizet: Variation 1, from the Prelude to *L'Arlésienne*
    (j) Copland: *Fanfare for the Common Man*

Assignment 2   Instruments from two sections of the orchestra are involved at the
beginning of each of these pieces:

    (a) Borodin: 'Dance of the Slave Girls', one of the Polovtsian Dances
        from his opera *Prince Igor*
    (b) Bizet: *The Carmen Ballet* (arranged by Shchedrin)
    (c) Grieg: 'Arab Dance', from *Peer Gynt*
    (d) Bruckner: Adagio from Symphony No. 7 in E major
    (e) Janáček: Sinfonietta

Assignment 3   **A** Name the four sections of the orchestra in the order in which you
hear them begin to play at the beginning of this piece:

     Sibelius: *Finlandia*

B In each of these pieces, the composer uses only three of the four
sections of the orchestra. As you listen, discover which section
is *missing*:

    (a) Bizet: Prelude to Act 2 ('Les Dragons d'Alcala'), from *Carmen*
    (b) Kodály: 'The Viennese Musical Clock', from *Háry János*

Project file

To help you with revision you will find it useful to start a project file in
which you can note down all the main points about the instruments of the
orchestra. To begin your file:

A Note down how the word *orchestra* took on its present meaning.

B Draw a diagram to show how the four sections of the orchestra are
arranged on the concert platform. Why do you think they are
positioned in this particular way?

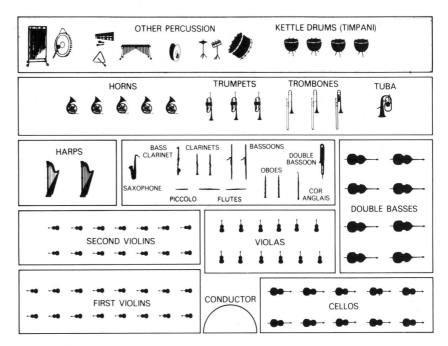

OTHER PERCUSSION KETTLE DRUMS (TIMPANI)

HORNS TRUMPETS TROMBONES TUBA

HARPS

BASS CLARINET CLARINETS BASSOONS
SAXOPHONE DOUBLE BASSOON
OBOES
PICCOLO FLUTES COR ANGLAIS

DOUBLE BASSES

SECOND VIOLINS VIOLAS

FIRST VIOLINS CONDUCTOR CELLOS

The Hallé Orchestra

2 Strings

Violin   Viola   Cello   Double bass   Harp

The strings are the 'backbone' of the orchestra. More than half
the members of an orchestra play string instruments, and so the
sound of the full orchestra is based upon a strong foundation of
string tone.

The string section of the orchestra consists of:

first violins	cellos
second violins	double basses
violas	harp

The violins of the orchestra are divided into two groups:
first violins and second violins. The difference is not in the
instruments themselves (which are exactly the same, of course)
but in the music they play – the first violins usually playing
higher notes than the seconds.

Violins, violas, cellos and double basses all produce their
sounds in exactly the same way. They may be played with a bow (a
wooden stick with horse-hair stretched tightly along it), or the
strings may be plucked with the finger-tips – an effect known as
pizzicato. The harp is always plucked. Although the harp may be
counted as a string instrument, its construction and the way in
which it is played rather set it apart from the other members of
the string section of the orchestra.

Violins, violas and cellos, though they differ in size, share
the same basic shape. Double basses are slightly different. They
have sloping shoulders, and the backs of these instruments are
flat rather than gently curved.

The string section is placed at the front of the orchestra. The
actual positioning of the separate groups of string instruments may
vary, but here is the arrangement which is most often seen:

There are often 16 first violins, 14 second violins, 12 violas, 10 cellos, and 8 double basses in a full orchestra. Notice how the number in each group gradually decreases - the lower the pitch of the instruments, the smaller the number needed to balance the sound.

Music to hear

A The five string variations from *The Young Person's Guide to the Orchestra,* by Benjamin Britten:
1 **Violins** - divided into the usual two groups, firsts and seconds, above a strongly rhythmic accompaniment mainly for brass
2 **Violas** - against crisp chords for woodwind and brass
3 **Cellos** - with an accompaniment in the style of a slow waltz
4 **Double basses** - accompanied by woodwind and tambourine
5 **Harp** - against a background of mysterious, rustling strings

B 'Dargason' from *St Paul's Suite for Strings,* by Gustav Holst
An old English dance-tune called the 'Dargason' threads its way from beginning to end of this lively piece. All the instruments take their turn to play it. On two occasions, another well-known English melody, 'Greensleeves', is smoothly woven into the music.

Project file

A Draw a diagram to show how the instruments of the string section are positioned on the concert platform. Make a note of why they are arranged in this way.

B 1 What is the difference between first violins and second violins?
2 Why are there fewer double basses than violins in an orchestra?
3 Make a note of the ways in which the harp differs from the other members of the string section.

Violin

(Italian: *violino*
French: *violon*
German: *Violine)*
Size: 59.4 cm
Range:

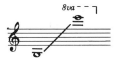

*13th-century musicians
playing two-stringed
rabab and lute*

Viol

There is a certain amount of mystery surrounding the origin of the violin. No one knows exactly when, or how, it was first invented. In medieval times, there was an amazing variety of bowed string instruments. The most important of these, which the violin might count among its ancestors, were: the Arabian *rabab* or 'spike-fiddle', which in Europe later became the *rebec* – slender, pear-shaped, and with usually three strings; and the five-stringed *fiddle* or *vielle,* shaped rather like a figure of eight.

The violin itself appeared, in Italy, at some time during the first half of the 16th century. At that time, the most popular bowed string instruments were the viols, but these were a completely separate family of string instruments, quite distinct from the violin.

For a time, viols and violins played side by side, but composers soon began to prefer the violin for its greater agility, power and brilliance of tone, and its much wider range of expression.

Gradually, the viols dropped out of use, until the present day, when they are once more being used to play music originally written for them.

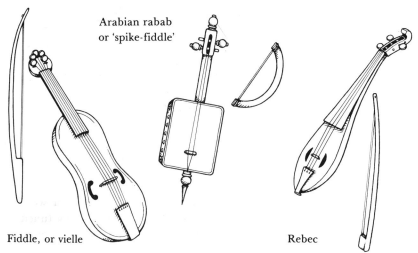

Arabian rabab
or 'spike-fiddle'

Fiddle, or vielle

Rebec

The violin, viola, cello and double bass produce their sounds in exactly the same way. Four strings - of gut, metal or nylon - are stretched across a hollow wooden body. The strings are fastened to the tail-piece, then taken across the bridge to the tuning-pegs. The bridge prevents the strings from touching the main body of the instrument, leaving them free to vibrate. The upper part of the body is usually made of pine, the rest of sycamore. Special varnish is applied to preserve the wood and to improve the quality of tone.

On this drawing, only the main parts are labelled - altogether, more than eighty separate parts go into the making of a violin.

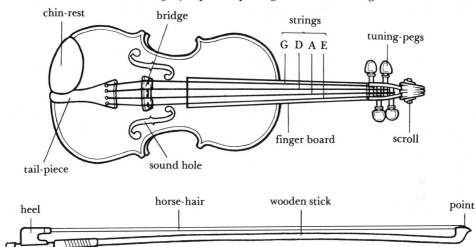

All sounds are caused by something vibrating. The slower the vibrations, the lower the note; the quicker the vibrations, the higher the note. In any instrument where the sounds are made by strings vibrating, the pitch of the notes depends on:

1	the length of the strings
2	the tension, or tightness, of the strings
3	the thickness of the strings

A longer string will vibrate more slowly than a shorter string, and so produce a lower note. But the shape and size of the violin make it necessary for all four strings to be of the same length. The strings produce notes of different pitch because they vary in tension and thickness. The player tunes the strings by adjusting the tuning-pegs. The tighter he makes a string, the higher it will sound. The four strings of the violin are tuned, a fifth apart, to these notes:

A thicker string will vibrate more slowly than a thinner string, producing a lower note. The string tuned to the note G is the thickest string; the E-string is the thinnest.

The player holds the violin so that it is tucked between his shoulder and the left side of his chin. Although the strings may be made to vibrate by plucking them with the finger-tips (*pizzicato*), the more usual way is by drawing the bow across them. This is a wooden stick with more than 200 strands of horse-hair stretched tightly along it. Before using the bow, the player rubs resin (usually pronounced 'rosin') onto the hair. This causes a certain stickiness, so that the hair 'catches' the string as the bow is drawn across, pulling it slightly to one side. The string immediately releases itself, but is caught again – and so the process is repeated, several times a second, causing the string to vibrate and so produce a note.

When a string is played, the vibrations travel by way of the bridge and the sound-post down into the hollow body of the instrument. The body itself vibrates, making the sounds both louder and richer before they flow out through the *f*-shaped sound-holes on either side of the bridge.

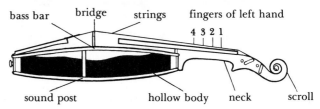

We have seen that the shorter a string is, the higher the note will sound. The size of the violin, of course, limits the length of the strings. The player cannot make them longer, but he can make different notes by *shortening* the strings. He does this by pressing them down to the finger-board. This is called 'stopping' the strings. When a string is stopped in this way, only the length from the bridge to the stopped point will vibrate.

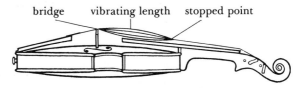

By stopping the strings at various points (the player is guided by ear alone, for there are no markings to show him where to place his fingers) a violinist can play up to fifty different notes.

Two notes can be sounded at the same time by stopping two strings at once. This is called double-stopping. Occasionally, the player is asked to play three notes at once (triple-stopping), or even four (quadruple-stopping), but in this case he must bow the lower two strings first, then quickly rock onto the higher two, since the curve of the bridge prevents the bow from being able to touch all four strings at once.

You may have seen a string-player, when he is not playing quick notes, rocking his left hand to and fro as he stops the strings. This is called *vibrato*. These rockings cause tiny variations in the pitch of a note, bringing life and warmth to the tone.

The violin has a tremendous range of expression. The sound can be made to grow gradually louder, or quieter. Notes can be played so that each is followed smoothly by the next, or they can be played crisply and quite separately. Loudness and tone may be varied by altering the pressure of the bow, the way in which it attacks or leaves the strings, or the actual positioning of the bow on the strings – close to the bridge, on or near the finger-board, or (as is most usual) midway between the two.

Here are some of the many ways in which the violin can be played, showing the extremely wide range of its sounds and tone-qualities:

legato (Italian for 'smoothly')   This is the most commonly used bowing-stroke, in which each note is followed smoothly by the next:

Mendelssohn : Violin Concerto in E minor

martellato (hammered)   The notes are bowed separately with short, vigorous strokes.

saltando (leaping)   Crisp, short strokes are made with the middle of the bow, causing it to bounce slightly on the string.

con sordino (with the mute)   A small comb-like device is clipped onto the bridge, dampening the vibrations and bringing a hushed, silvery quality to the tone. When the composer wants the player to remove the mute, he writes on the music the Italian words *senza sordino* (without the mute).

Tchaikovsky : Violin Concerto in D major

pizzicato   The strings are plucked with the finger-tips. When the composer wants the player to use the bow again, he writes the word *arco* (bow).

tremolo (trembling)   There are two kinds of tremolo:
   fingered tremolo – the swift alternation of two notes, each group of notes taken with a single stroke of the bow;
   bowed tremolo – an agitated, rather dramatic, quivering effect consisting of quick repetitions of a note by making very rapid up-and-down movements of the bow.

sul ponticello (on the bridge)   The strings are bowed very close to the bridge, producing a rather eerie sound, especially when combined with bowed tremolo.

harmonics   These are high, soft, flute-like sounds caused by touching a string lightly with the finger-tip.

col legno (with the wood)   The player turns his bow over and uses the wooden part on the strings instead of the horse-hair.

Although minor alterations have been made over the years in the construction and size of the violin (including the design of the bow) it has changed surprisingly little since the 16th century.

Some of the finest violins were made during the 17th century by three families of superb craftsmen, all living in the same town of Cremona in Northern Italy: the Amati, Guarneri, and Stradivari families. The greatest of these Italian violin-makers was Antonio Stradivari. He is known to have made more than 1000 instruments (including violas and cellos as well as violins), many of which are still played all over the world today.

The picture on the left shows his famous 'Messiah' violin – so called because of its finely carved tail-piece which shows Jesus lying in the manger. Below is the label he fixed inside the violin, giving the year when it was made (1716). Naturally, a violin by Stradivari is extremely valuable. One of his lesser-known violins fetched £145,000 recently at auction.

The 'Messiah' violin from the Ashmolean Museum, Oxford

Music to hear

For unaccompanied violin
    Bach: Gavotte, from Partita No. 3 in E major
    Paganini: *Caprices* (especially No. 24, the tune of which has been taken as a theme for variations by many other composers)
    Bartók: Sonata – the third movement in particular

For violin and keyboard
    Tartini: Sonata in G minor, 'The Devil's Trill'
    Beethoven: first movement from the 'Kreutzer' Sonata
    Penderecki: *Three Miniatures* for violin and piano
    Jazz pieces played by Stéphane Grappelli and Yehudi Menuhin

For solo violin and orchestra
    Vivaldi: *The Four Seasons*
    Concertos by Bach, Mozart, Beethoven, Mendelssohn, Brahms, Bruch, Tchaikovsky, Sibelius, Bartók, Berg and Penderecki
    Sarasate: *Zigeunerweisen* (Gypsy Melodies)

For the violin section of the orchestra
    Britten: Variations 3: 'Romance'; 4: 'Aria Italiana'; and 5: 'Bourrée Classique', from *Variations on a Theme of Frank Bridge*
    Rimsky-Korsakov: *The Flight of the Bumble Bee*

Assignment 4 **A** Give the meaning of each of these terms describing special ways of playing string instruments. In each case, explain how the effect is produced:

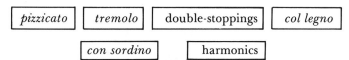

| *pizzicato* | *tremolo* | double-stoppings | *col legno* |

| *con sordino* | harmonics |

B Match each of the special ways of playing the violin, recorded on the cassette, to one of the terms in the boxes above.

Assignment 5 Explain each of these Italian terms connected with string-playing:
(a) *arco* (b) *legato* (c) *vibrato* (d) *sul ponticello* (e) *senza sordino*

Assignment 6 From the boxes below, find two famous violin-makers, together with the town in which they lived; and three well-known violinists, one of them also a composer:

| Menuhin | Amati | Paganini | Oistrakh | Cremona | Stradivari |

Project file

A Make a copy of this drawing of a violin and bow, but instead of numbers, add the correct name for each part indicated.

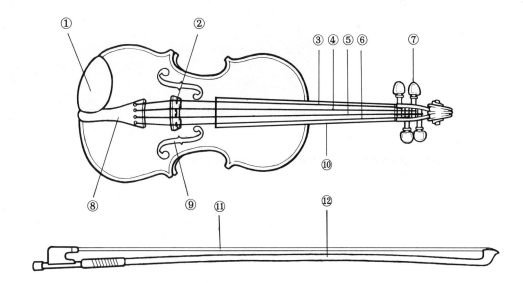

B How does the violin produce its basic sound? Describe how the different notes are made, and how the vibrations of the strings are amplified and made richer.

C What about the ancestors of the violin? Make notes on them, perhaps including drawings as well.

Almost all the points mentioned in connection with the violin apply equally to the viola, cello, and double bass. Basically, these differ from the violin only in size, range of notes and tone-qualities. In fact in earlier times all four of these string instruments were usually referred to merely as 'violins'. For instance, during the 17th century, the famous string orchestra at the court of Louis XIV (the 'Sun King' of France) was known as *les vingt-quatre violons du Roy* ('the King's twenty-four violins'). In time, though, the three larger instruments took on the separate names by which we know them today: viola, cello, and double bass.

Viola

(I: *viola*
F: *alto,* or
viole
G: *Bratsche*)
Size: 69.2 cm
Range:

Violin   Viola

The viola is a seventh larger than the violin, and is slightly heavier. Like the violin, it is tucked under the chin to be played but due to the extra length of the instrument the player's left arm is generally held straighter, more extended. And the distances between the notes, where the player 'stops' the strings, are slightly greater. The four strings are longer and thicker than the violin's and are tuned a fifth lower, to these notes:

C   G   D   A   C   G   D   A

Notice that the higher three strings of the viola are tuned to the same notes as the lower three strings of the violin. But only the highest viola notes are written in the treble clef. Most of the notes played by the viola fit very conveniently onto the alto (or 'C') clef, in which the middle line of the stave is middle C:

middle C →

Although longer than the violin, the viola is still comparatively small in size, taking into account the deepness of its pitch. This, together with the fact that its strings are slightly thicker, makes the tone generally darker, less brilliant, than that of the violin – even when playing notes of exactly the same pitch. Higher notes tend to sound rather thin and reedy, but the tone-quality in the lower and middle parts of the viola's range is warm, dark and rich:

'Song', from *Háry János*, by Kodály

The differing tone-qualities of the violin and viola are clearly heard in this melody from Mozart's Sinfonia Concertante (K364):

Until Mozart's time, the viola mostly filled in middle notes of the harmonies, or doubled the notes already given to the cellos. But during the 19th century, composers began to make the viola parts of their scores more adventurous and far more interesting to play.

Music to hear

For viola and piano
   Hindemith: first movement from Sonata Opus 11 No. 4

For solo viola with orchestra
   Bach: Brandenburg Concerto No. 6 (including two solo violas)
   Berlioz: 'March of the Pilgrims', from *Harold in Italy*
   Howells: *Elegy* for viola, string quartet and string orchestra
   Viola Concertos by Walton and Hindemith (*Der Schwanendreher*)

Orchestral solos for viola
   Adam: Pas de Deux, from the ballet *Giselle*
   Britten: opening of the Passacaglia, from *Peter Grimes*

For the viola section of the orchestra
   Copland: middle section of 'Saturday Night Waltz', from *Rodeo*
   Bartók: 'Interrupted Intermezzo', from *Concerto for Orchestra*
   Rimsky-Korsakov: third movement of the Suite *'The Golden Cockerel'*

For solo violin, solo viola and orchestra
   Mozart: Sinfonia Concertante (K364)

Cello

(I: *violoncello*
F: *violoncelle*
G: *Violoncell*)
Size: 1.23 m
Range:

The correct name for this instrument is really, as in Italian, violoncello – but it is always called cello (pronounced 'chello') for short. It is far too big, of course, to tuck under the chin like the violin or the viola. Instead, it is held lightly between the knees, resting on the floor by means of an adjustable metal spike.

The four strings of the cello are tuned in fifths, one octave below the viola, to these notes:

C   G   D   A

The cello has the widest dynamic range, soft to loud, of all the string instruments; and an extremely wide range of notes, covering almost four octaves. Lower notes are written in the bass clef; higher notes in the tenor, or even treble clef:

middle C →

bass clef   tenor clef   treble clef

The longer, thicker strings and larger body of the cello produce a sound which can be full and penetrating. The tone-quality is gloriously warm and rich:

Schumann: Cello Concerto in A minor

fp

In spite of its size, the cello can be quite agile when given a fast, rhythmic tune to play.

Music to hear   For unaccompanied cello
   Bach: Bourrées , from Suites No. 3 in C major
   Kódaly: Sonata, Opus 8

For cello with piano
   Saint-Saëns: 'The Swan', from *The Carnival of Animals*
   Britten: 'Dialogo' and 'Scherzo-pizzicato', from Sonata in C, Opus 65

18

For solo cello and orchestra
  Concertos by Haydn, Schumann, Dvořák, Elgar, Shostakovich
  Tchaikovsky: *Variations on a Rococo Theme*
  Lloyd-Webber: *Variations* (on a theme of Paganini)

For the cello section of the orchestra
  Schubert: first movement, second theme from the 'Unfinished'
    Symphony
  Brahms: third movement from Symphony No. 3 in F major

For violin, cello and orchestra
  Brahms: Double Concerto in A minor

Double bass

(I: *contrabasso,*
    or *violone*
 F: *contrebasse*
 G: *Kontrabass*)
Size: 1.85 m
Range:

The double bass, sometimes just called bass for short, is much bigger than the cello, so the strings are longer, and thicker still. Distances which the hand must stretch to find the different notes are correspondingly greater. The player must either stand, or perch upon the edge of a high stool.

The double bass is slightly different in shape from the violin, viola and cello. The back is flatter, and the shoulders slope more – two characteristics from the older family of viols which, in this case, conveniently allow the player to 'lean round' the instrument to play it.

Originally, double basses had only three strings, but nowadays they have four, sometimes five, the fifth string reaching down to low C so that the range then lies exactly one octave below that of the cello.

Music for double bass is written in the bass clef, but one octave higher than the notes actually sound. This avoids too many leger lines below the stave. Unlike the violin, viola and cello, which are tuned in fifths, the double bass is tuned in fourths:

actual
sounds:

(C) E A D G

...but
written
down as:

(C) E A D G

19

The double bass is rarely given solos. It is less agile than the other string instruments; and the strings are very thick, producing a gruff, dry, rather buzzy sound when played with the bow:

Saint-Saëns: 'The Elephant', from *Carnival of the Animals*

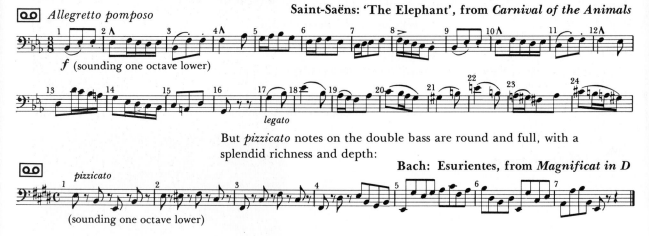

f (sounding one octave lower)

legato

But *pizzicato* notes on the double bass are round and full, with a splendid richness and depth:

Bach: **Esurientes, from** *Magnificat in D*

(sounding one octave lower)

The double basses give depth and resonance to the string section and indeed to the whole orchestra. Until the end of the 19th century they usually doubled the cello part, one octave lower, but holding the bass-line if the cellos were given a melody. Modern composers, however, often write independent parts for cellos and double basses.

Music to hear

For solo double bass and orchestra
    Dittersdorf: Concerto in E major; Sinfonia Concertante (with viola)

Orchestral solos for double bass
    Mahler: third movement from Symphony No. 1 in D major
    Prokofiev: Romance, from *Lieutenant Kijé*
    Stravinsky: Vivo, from *Pulcinella* (a comic duet with trombone)

For the double bass section of the orchestra (with cellos)
    Beethoven: first part of the Finale of Symphony No. 9 ('Choral')

The double bass in jazz
    Recordings featuring performances by Charlie Mingus

Harp

(I: *arpa*
F: *harpe*
G: *Harfe*)
Range:

The harp is one of the oldest of all instruments, probably origi-nating in the twang of a hunting-bow. Early harps had few strings; but the modern harp has 47 strings, graded in length.

The harpist does not have to 'stop' his strings to find the notes as, for instance, a violinist. But he must make sure that each string is perfectly in tune before playing. This takes quite a time, and the harpist usually arrives on the platform long before a concert is due to begin in order to tune his strings.

From middle C upwards, the strings are now usually made of nylon. The lower strings are made of gut, the eleven lowest being wound with wire. To help the harpist to locate the correct strings, all the unwound C-strings are coloured red, and the F-strings blue.

Medieval harp

You may wonder how 47 strings manage to cover the wide range of notes which the harp can play. At the base of the harp there are seven pedals, one for each note of the octave – a pedal for all the A-strings, another for the B-strings, and so on.

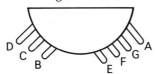

left foot   right foot

Each pedal has three notches, so it can quickly adjust the length of its strings to give any one of three different notes. Taking the C-pedal as an example: in the higher position, all the C-strings sound the note C flat at varying octaves. Pressing the pedal down a notch shortens the strings slightly, so they now sound C natural. Pressing the pedal down into the lowest notch gives C sharp.

A harpist may pluck single notes; or play a melody, providing an accompaniment at the same time. But the most characteristic sounds of the orchestral harp are chords (with the notes either 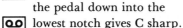 plucked together or spread out one after the other as *arpeggios*) and the *glissando* (Italian for 'sliding') in which the player sweeps the fingers swiftly across the strings.

The player may pluck the strings near the sound-board, giving a rather thin, drier sound; or play harmonics – these mysterious, haunting sounds are made by placing the side of the hand lightly against the middle of a string, and plucking the top half only.

Music to hear

Unaccompanied harp sounds
     Ravel: the cadenza from *Introduction and Allegro*

Solo harp with orchestra
     Debussy: *Danse sacrée et danse profane,* for harp and strings
     Alwyn: *Lyra Angelica,* for harp and string orchestra

Orchestral use
     Solo – Tchaikovsky: 'Waltz of the Flowers', from the *Nutcracker* Suite
     Accompaniment – Franck: slow movement from Symphony in D minor
                 Bizet: Prélude to Act 3 of *Carmen*

<table>
<tr><td>**Music to hear
for strings**</td><td>The string section of the orchestra also exists as a separate unit
in its own right, known as the 'string orchestra':</td></tr>
</table>

Mozart: *Eine Kleine Nachtmusik*
Dvořák: Serenade for String Orchestra in E major
Vaughan Williams: *Fantasia on a Theme of Thomas Tallis* (String
    forces required here are two string orchestras - one large, one
    small - and a string quartet: two violins, viola, and cello.)
Penderecki: *Threnody – To the Victims of Hiroshima* (In this piece,
    Penderecki draws new sounds from string instruments. For many
    of them, he had to devise new ways of writing down the music.)

Assignment 7

Identify the string instruments which play the seven extracts of
music recorded on the cassette.

Assignment 8

Name the instruments from the string section of the orchestra which
play the tune at the beginning of each of these pieces:

(a) Prokofiev: Romeo at Juliet's Tomb
(b) Tchaikovsky: second movement from Symphony No. 6 ('Pathétique')
(c) Bartók: *Music for Strings, Percussion and Celesta*
(d) Shostakovich: second movement from Symphony No. 5 in D minor
(e) Kodály: Intermezzo from *Háry János*

Assignment 9

As you listen to the beginning of each of these pieces, choose the
correct term from the boxes to describe the special way in which
the instruments from the string section are being played:

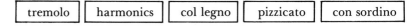

| tremolo | harmonics | col legno | pizzicato | con sordino |

(a) Tchaikovsky: third movement from Symphony No. 4 in F minor
(b) Mahler: Symphony No. 1 in D major
(c) Grieg: 'The Death of Åse', from *Peer Gynt*
(d) Stravinsky: the end of Berceuse and into Finale from *The Firebird*
(e) Rachmaninov: Variation 9, from *Rhapsody on a Theme of Paganini*
(f) Borodin: *In the Steppes of Central Asia*
(g) Mussorgsky: 'Cum mortuis in lingua mortua', the second part of
    'Catacombs', from *Pictures at an Exhibition*
(h) Franck: slow movement from Symphony in D minor
(i) Beethoven: slow movement from Piano Concerto No. 5 ('Emperor')
(j) Holst: 'Mars, the Bringer of War', from *The Planets*
(k) Falla: *Nights in the Gardens of Spain*

Assignment 10

from Symphony No. 1 by Brahms

Write out the above snatch of melody:
(a) in the alto (or 'C') clef, to be played by a viola;
(b) in the tenor clef, to be played by a cello;

(c) one octave lower, in the bass clef, to be played by a double bass; then write out the tune again, showing the actual sounds the double bass will produce.

Assignment 11

Listen to Variation 6: 'Wiener Walzer' (Viennese Waltz) from *Variations on a Theme of Frank Bridge*, by Benjamin Britten.

This piece divides into three sections. In the first section:

(a) Are the double basses played *arco*, or *pizzicato?*
(b) Which instruments play the tune in this unusual Waltz?

In the slower middle section of the piece:

(c) Which instruments are played *pizzicato?*
(d) Which instrument later plays a solo? Is it a viola, a cello, or a double bass?

The third section begins with a trill on double basses followed by two *pizzicato* chords. Then the Waltz begins again:

(e) Which Italian words describe the way the accompaniment is played?
(f) Which Italian words describe the way the Waltz-tune is played?
(g) Is the final chord of the piece played *arco*, or *pizzicato?*

Assignment 12

Still from Britten's *Variations on a Theme of Frank Bridge*, describe how the strings are played at the beginning of:

(a) the Introduction
(b) Variation 7: 'Moto Perpetuo'
(c) Variation 9: 'Chant'

Project file

A What are the differences in range and tone-quality between the instruments in each of these pairs?

| violin : viola | | cello : double bass |

B Although the four strings of a violin are of equal length, they sound four different notes. What are the reasons for this?

C 1. Note the meaning of each of these terms connected with harp-playing:

| arpeggios | | glissando | | harmonics |

2. How do you get 80 or so notes from the harp, which has only 47 strings?

D *Research* Find out which string instrument is associated with each of these famous performers:

Josef Joachim	Domenico Dragonetti	Marisa Robles
Lionel Tertis	Msitislav Rostropovich	Julian Lloyd-Webber
Ossian Ellis	William Primrose	Itzhak Perlman
Pablo Casals	Kyung Wha-Chung	Gary Karr

3 Woodwind

As the name 'woodwind' suggests, the instruments of this section of the orchestra are mostly made of wood, though flutes and piccolos are now often made of metal instead. The sounds are caused by the player's breath – either by setting a reed vibrating or, in the case of the flute and piccolo, by blowing across an oval-shaped hole. In each case, a column of air is made to vibrate inside a hollow tube. The length of the air column determines the pitch:

> the shorter the air column, the higher the note
> the longer the air column, the lower the note

(Compare this with the sounds of instruments in the string section: the shorter strings of the violin produce relatively high notes; the longer strings of the double bass produce much lower notes.)

| Double bassoon | Bassoon | Clarinet | Bass clarinet | Tenor saxophone | Oboe | Cor anglais | Flute | Piccolo |

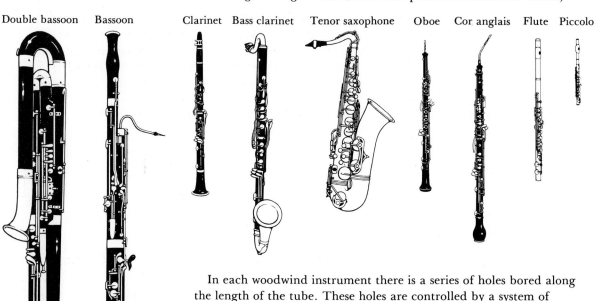

In each woodwind instrument there is a series of holes bored along the length of the tube. These holes are controlled by a system of keys, springs and levers, some of them controlling holes which would otherwise be beyond easy reach of the player's fingers. When all the holes are covered, the instrument sounds its lowest note. But if the player uncovers the bottom hole, allowing air to escape through it, the vibrating length of the column of air inside the tube is shortened, and so a higher note is sounded:

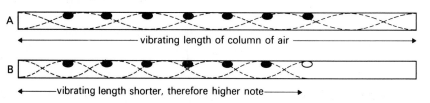

A ⟷ vibrating length of column of air ⟶

B ⟷ vibrating length shorter, therefore higher note ⟶

Flutes, oboes and bassoons produce notes an octave higher by what is called 'over-blowing'. The player uncovers a small hole called a 'vent' to let air in at a certain point. This prevents the air column from vibrating as a whole, and so a higher note is sounded. Clarinets produce notes a twelfth higher when over-blown in this way.

At the end of the 18th century - when Haydn was writing his last symphonies and Beethoven was about to write his first - the woodwind section consisted of 2 flutes, 2 oboes, 2 clarinets and 2 bassoons. During the 19th century, a larger or smaller version of each of these main instruments became generally accepted into the orchestra, increasing the range of notes and variety of tone-colours, so that the woodwind section of the modern orchestra often includes:

> flutes and piccolo
> oboes and cor anglais
> clarinets and bass clarinet
> (and occasionally saxophone)
> bassoons and double bassoon

Whereas the sounds of the string section blend together, those of the woodwind are more distinctive and individual, tending to contrast rather than blend. In the string section, several instruments of the same type play the same music, but each woodwind player has his own part to play. Woodwind instruments are frequently given solos, so this section is placed in the centre of the orchestra, raised higher than the strings, and directly in front of the conductor:

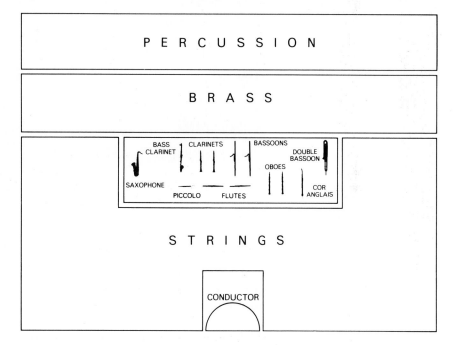

Music to hear

The four woodwind variations from *The Young Person's Guide to the Orchestra,* by Benjamin Britten:
1 **Flutes and piccolos** - chirruping and fluttering above first and second violins (played *tremolo*), harp and triangle
2 **Oboes** - playing smooth, plaintive phrases, accompanied by lower strings and hushed rolls on a kettle drum

3 Clarinets – in a game of musical leap-frog, accompanied by *pizzicato* strings and tuba

4 Bassoons – playing a mock-solemn march against a crisp accompaniment for strings and snare drum (but with the snares lifted away from the drum-skin)

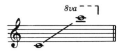

Project file

A Write down how woodwind instruments make their sounds.

B Draw a diagram to show how the instruments of the woodwind section are arranged on the concert platform. Why are they given this central position in the orchestra?

Flute

(I: *flauto*
F: *flûte*
G: *Flöte)*
Size: 68'cm
Range:

It is easy to recognise the flute among the instruments of the woodwind section, as it is held sideways rather than straight in front of the player. There is no reed. The sounds are produced by what is called 'edge-tone'. The player directs a stream of air across an oval-shaped hole cut about 7 cm from the sealed end of the instrument (the other end being left open). This mouth-hole is placed just below the player's lower lip. The farther edge of the mouth-hole splits the stream of air, causing the air column inside the instrument to vibrate and so produce a note. (You can get a similar effect by blowing across a pen-top or bottle.)

The recorder – an 'end-blown' flute

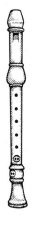

The first flutes to be used in the orchestra were held vertically and 'end-blown'. These included recorders. The 'side-blown' or 'transverse' flute (basically the flute we know today but with fewer keys) joined the orchestra around the middle of the 17th century. For a time, both end-blown and side-blown flutes were used, though rarely in the same music. But by the middle of the 18th century, the side-blown flute had completely taken over, due to its greater expressiveness, power, and variety of tone.

The higher notes of the flute are clear, cool and penetrating:

The lower notes are soft, warm and mellow, often with a haunting 'liquid' quality. The difference in tone between the lower and higher registers of the flute can be clearly heard at the beginning of Poulenc's Flute Sonata.

A flautist can play notes smoothly in succession, or, by making the letters 't-k-t-k' with his tongue, he can give each note a crisp attack. One rather strange effect the flautist can produce is called 'flutter-tonguing', in which he rolls a letter 'r' as he blows. This sound can be heard during the second part of Berio's *Sequenza for Solo Flute*.

Music to hear

For unaccompanied flute
   Debussy: *Syrinx* (contrast of high and low registers)
   Varèse: *Density 21.5*

For flute and keyboard
   Handel: Flute Sonatas from Opus 1, especially Nos. 5 and 9
   Poulenc: Flute Sonata

For solo flute and orchestra
   Bach: Dances from Orchestral Suite No. 2 in B minor
   Mozart: Flute Concertos; Concerto for Flute and Harp (K299)
   Nielsen: Allegretto, from Flute Concerto

Orchestral solos for flute
   Bizet: Prelude to Act 3 of *Carmen*
   Sibelius: 'Nocturne', and 'Khadra's Dance', from *Belshazzar's Feast*
   Bizet: 'Danse Bohème', from *Carmen* (2 flutes)
   Tchaikovsky: 'Dance of the Flutes', from the *Nutcracker* Suite (3 flutes)

Piccolo

(I: *flauto piccolo*
F: *petite flûte*
G: *kleine Flöte*)
Size: 32 cm
Range:

Piccolo simply means 'small', and the piccolo is really a half-sized flute. As the method of fingering is exactly the same, all flautists are equally able to play the piccolo. The range lies an octave higher than the flute, and the upper notes are piercingly brilliant. To avoid a great many leger lines above the stave, music for piccolo is written one octave lower than it actually sounds.

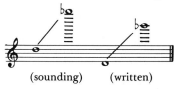

(sounding)   (written)

from *Lieutenant Kijé*, by Prokofiev

(sounding one octave higher)

The piccolo is easily heard above the sound of the full orchestra but, because of the shrillness of its tone, composers use it very sparingly. It is played by the second (or third) flautist, who interchanges flute with piccolo as and when the music requires.

Music to hear

Pierné: 'The Entrance of the Little Fauns', from *Cydalise*
Sousa: *The Stars and Stripes Forever* (repeat of the third tune)
Arnold: English Dance No. 5
Stravinsky: 'Dance of the Firebird', from the ballet *The Firebird*
Tchaikovsky: 'Chinese Dance', from the *Nutcracker* Suite (for two flutes and piccolo)

Two other types of flute are sometimes now used in the orchestra. The first of these used to be called the bass flute, with a range lying four notes below that of the ordinary flute. But a still larger flute, playing a whole octave lower, is sometimes now used, especially in 'pop' music, and music for films and television. Due to its larger size the latter now takes the name of bass flute, while musicians tend to refer to the former as the alto flute.

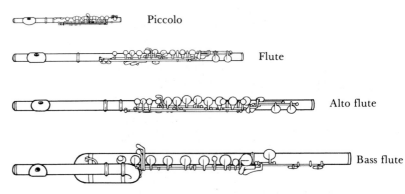

Piccolo

Flute

Alto flute

Bass flute

Oboe

(I: *oboe*
F: *hautbois*
G: *Hoboe*)
Size: 64.8 cm
Range:

The oboe has a double reed. A strip of thin cane is folded double, then bound round a small metal tube called the staple. The fold in the doubled reed is cut, and the ends finely tapered. The staple fits into a cork base which fixes firmly into the top of the oboe.

The oboist rests the tip of the double reed between his lips, drawing them back slightly over his teeth. He directs a steady stream of air between the two reeds, making them vibrate against each other (in a similar manner to the edges of a folded leaf held between the thumbs and blown). The vibration of the two reeds sets the air column inside the oboe vibrating, so producing a note.

The lower notes of the oboe are rich; the higher notes thinner and more penetrating. The sound is more 'tangy', obviously reedier when compared with the clear, open tone-quality of the flute:

Grieg: 'Morning', from *Peer Gynt*

28

The oboe has a smaller range of notes than the other main woodwind instruments, but is capable of great variation of tone and style of playing. In slow melodies, it tends to sound rather melancholy:

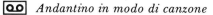 *Andantino in modo di canzone*

from Symphony No.4 in F minor, by Tchaikovsky

But it can play lively, chattering tunes extremely crisply, with a splendid edge and bite to the tone. Because of its penetrating sound it is the oboe which, before a concert begins, plays the note A to which all the other players tune their instruments.

Oboes joined the orchestra around the middle of the 17th century.

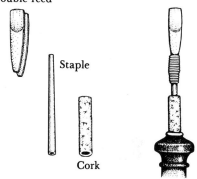

Double reed

Staple

Cork

Music to hear

For unaccompanied oboe
> Britten: *Six Metamorphoses after Ovid,* Opus 49
> Berio: *Sequenza VII for Solo Oboe*

For oboe and piano
> Poulenc: Scherzo and 'Déploration' (Lament) from Oboe Sonata

For solo oboe with orchestra
> Concertos by Handel, Marcello, Richard Strauss, Vaughan Williams,
> and Henze (Double Concerto for oboe, harp and 18 solo strings)

Orchestral solos for oboe:
> Tchaikovsky: 'Scène', from *Swan Lake* (Introduction to Act 2)
> Delius: 'La Calinda', from the opera *Koanga*
> Handel: 'Arrival of the Queen of Sheba', from *Solomon* (for 2 oboes)

Cor anglais

(I: *corno inglese*
F: *cor anglais*
G: *englisches Horn)*
Size: 80 cm
Range:

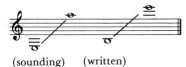

(sounding)   (written)

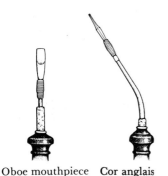

Oboe mouthpiece   Cor anglais
and reed   crook and reed

**'Transposing'
instruments**

Oboe   Cor anglais

The name means – and this instrument is sometimes called – 'English horn'. This is strange, as the cor anglais is not English in origin, neither is it a horn. It is instead a larger, alto, oboe. It has been suggested that *anglais* is really a mis-spelling of the French word *anglé,* meaning 'angled', and referring to the way in which the crook (the mouth-piece in which the double reed is fixed) is bent back to meet the player's lips. In fact, in early models the entire instrument was curved in the shape of an animal's horn to allow the player's fingers to reach the holes easily.

The notes sounded by the cor anglais are not, in fact, the same as those which are actually written down for it to play. This requires some explanation.

There are, in fact, several instruments in the orchestra whose music is written down at a different pitch from that of the actual sounds when the notes are played. We call these 'transposing' instruments. There is always a good reason why the notes are written in such a way – usually to make things more straightforward for the player himself. We saw earlier on that music for double bass is written one octave higher than it actually sounds; and that music for piccolo is written one octave lower. In both these cases, this is to avoid a great many leger lines below or above the stave. In the case of the cor anglais, however, it is not a simple octave transposition.

The pitch of the cor anglais lies five notes lower than that of the oboe. The method of fingering is exactly the same on both instruments, so all oboists are equally able to play the cor anglais. Therefore, to make things straightforward for the player, in cor anglais music all the notes are written five notes higher than they actually sound. This means the player reads, and fingers, the notes exactly as if they were written for oboe, but they automatically sound a fifth lower at the correct pitch for cor anglais.

For example, if the player places his fingers so that on an oboe they would produce the note D, on the cor anglais the G below is sounded instead:

oboe:

cor anglais, written:

... but sounding:

Like the oboe, the cor anglais has a double reed. The bell of the instrument is pear-shaped, closing round so that the aperture is rather small. This makes the tone-quality softer, richer, even more plaintive than that of the oboe, admirably suiting the cor anglais to smooth melodies which have a tinge of sadness about them:

Dvořák: Sympony No.9 ('From the New World')

Largo

p (sounding a fifth lower)

Music to hear

For solo cor anglais and orchestra
    Donizetti: Concertino in G major
    William Alwyn: *Autumn Legend*

Orchestral solos for cor anglais
    Franck: slow movement from Symphony in D minor
    Sibelius: *The Swan of Tuonela*
    Borodin: 'Dance of the Maidens', one of the Polovtsian Dances from
        Prince Igor (a good chance to compare the tone-qualities of oboe and
        cor anglais)

Assignment 13

| flute | piccolo | oboe | cor anglais |

In which order are these woodwind instruments heard in the eight extracts of music recorded on the cassette?

Project file

A   What are the important differences between the flute and the oboe, especially in the ways in which their sounds are made?

B   Why is:
1. music for piccolo written an octave lower than it sounds?
2. music for cor anglais written a fifth higher than it sounds?

C   *Research* Find out why the name Boehm is important to flute and oboe players.

Clarinet

(I: *clarinetto*
F: *clarinette*
G: *Klarinette)*

Size:
B flat clarinet: 66.7 cm
A clarinet: 69.8 cm
Range:

B flat clarinet

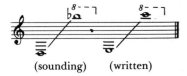

(sounding)   (written)

A clarinet

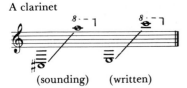

(sounding)   (written)

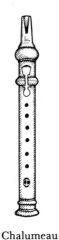

Chalumeau

Of the four main woodwind instruments, the clarinet was last to join the orchestra. It was invented around 1690 by Johann Denner, a Nuremberg instrument-maker, who made improvements to the instrument known as the *chalumeau*. He named his new instrument clarinet because the higher notes seemed similar in brilliance to the high-pitched trumpet, whose Italian name was *clarino*. It was a century, though, before the clarinet gained a firm place in the orchestra.

The clarinet has a single reed – a flat piece of cane, shaved to delicate thinness at the end – which fits over an oblong hole in the wedge-shaped mouth-piece. The reed is held in place by a metal band with adjustable screws, called the ligature.

The clarinettist takes the tip of the mouth-piece, reed downwards, between his lips, curling his lower lip back slightly over his teeth to make a cushion for the reed. He closes his mouth around the mouth-piece to prevent air from escaping. As he blows, air passes between the mouth-piece and the reed, causing it to vibrate.

This sets the air column vibrating inside the clarinet, and so produces a note. Whereas the tube of the oboe is conical in shape, the clarinet's is mainly cylindrical. The effect of this is that the sounds it produces are low in relation to its length.

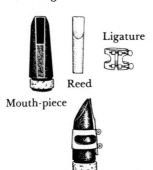

Ligature

Reed

Mouth-piece

Clarinets were originally made in three sizes: pitched in C, in B flat, and in A. (The clarinet in C eventually fell out of use due to the superior tone of the other two.) For the convenience of the player, music was written out in such a way that the fingering was always exactly the same, regardless of which clarinet was used. But this meant that while notes for clarinet in C actually sounded as written, those for clarinets in B flat or A had to be written higher in order to sound at the required pitch. In fact, these are examples of the 'transposing' instruments mentioned on page 30.

The clarinet in B flat *sounds* the note B flat when the note C is *written*. To sound the note C, D must be written. So all notes for this clarinet must be written a tone higher than they are to sound

The clarinet in A *sounds* the note A when the written note is C. And so all notes for this clarinet must be written a minor third (or three semitones) higher than they are to sound.

The choice of which clarinet, B flat or A, is to be used is in fact made by the composer, who decides which of the two would have fewest flats or sharps when the music is written out:

Actual sounds:

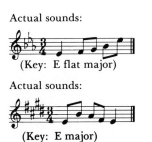

(Key: E flat major)

If written for clarinet in B flat, a tone higher:

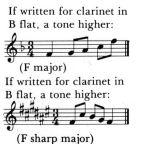

(F major)

If written for clarinet in A, a minor third higher:

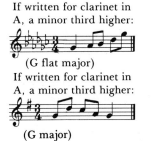

(G flat major)

(In this instance, the clarinet in B flat would be used)

Actual sounds:

(Key: E major)

If written for clarinet in B flat, a tone higher:

(F sharp major)

If written for clarinet in A, a minor third higher:

(G major)

(Here, the clarinet in A would be used)

The player takes up the clarinet indicated and fingers the notes as written. According to the type of clarinet and the transposition, the sounds automatically come out in the correct key and at the correct pitch to match those of the other instruments playing.

Of all woodwind instruments, the clarinet has the widest range of notes. The tone-quality, less reedy than that of the oboe, varies according to register. The lower notes, those below middle C, are called the *chalumeau* register. These are rich, rather hollow yet velvety. Notes in the middle register are rather brighter, and increase in brilliance as they go into the higher register where the sounds can be quite piercing, sometimes strident.

The clarinettist has great control over expression and dynamics, playing sudden crescendos and diminuendos with ease. The clarinet is equally suited to smooth, expressive melodies or quick, rhythmic tunes. It can be extremely agile, taking wide leaps with little difficulty. Swift, bubbling arpeggios are particularly effective.

from *Dances of Galanta*, by Kodály

(clarinet in A, actual sounds)

Music to hear

For unaccompanied clarinet
Stravinsky: *Three Pieces* for Clarinet Solo (particularly No. 2)

For clarinet and piano
Poulenc: second and third movements from Clarinet Sonata

For solo clarinet and orchestra
Concertos by Mozart: Nielsen (opening and cadenza); Finzi (Rondo)
Stravinsky: *Ebony Concerto* (for jazz clarinettist Woody Herman)

For clarinet and string quartet
Clarinet Quintets by Mozart, Brahms, Reger, Bliss (third movement)

Orchestral solos for clarinet
Respighi: 'The Pines of the Janiculum', from *The Pines of Rome*
Tchaikovsky: opening of Symphony No. 5 (2 clarinets, low register)
Mozart: Trio of Symphony No. 39 (2 clarinets: one low, one high)

The clarinet in jazz
Pieces featuring Johnny Dodds, Benny Goodman, Artie Shaw

Bass clarinet

(I: *clarinetto basso*
F: *clarinette basse*
G: *Bassklarinette*)
Size: 1.4 m
Range:

(sounding)   (written)

The bass clarinet is twice as long as the normal clarinet, and is pitched an octave lower. The top part of the instrument curves backwards so that the player can easily reach the mouth-piece with its single reed. The bottom end flares into an upturned metal bell.

When needed, the bass clarinet is played by the third clarinettist. To makes things easier for the player, notes are usually written in the treble clef, an octave and a tone higher than they will actually sound.

The tone of the bass clarinet is smooth, spendidly rich and resonant, but with a rather hollow, 'woody' quality.

Music to hear

Alois Hàba: Suite for Solo Bass Clarinet
Sibelius: middle section of 'Khadra's Dance', from *Belshazzar's Feast*
Wagner: Scene 3 from Act 2 of *Tristan and Isolde*
Delius: Prelude to *Irmelin* (brief solos near the beginning and end)

Two other kinds of clarinet are sometimes used in the orchestra. The small E-flat clarinet has a high-pitched, shrill sound, clearly heard at the end of Strauss's *Till Eulenspiegel*, imitating Till's shrieks of terror as he is hanged. In the final movement, 'Dream of a Witches' Sabbath', from Berlioz's *Symphonie Fantastique* it suggests the fiendish cackling of a witch as she rides her broomstick.

There is also a contrabass (or 'double bass') clarinet, rarely used, which sounds an octave lower than the bass clarinet, two octaves below the normal clarinet.

Saxophone

(I: *saxofono*
or *sassofono*
F: *saxophone*
G: *saxophon*)
Range:

(written notes – sounding a major
6th lower for E flat alto
saxophone; an octave and a tone
lower for B flat tenor saxophone)

The saxophone was invented during the 1840s by a Belgian clarinettist and instrument-maker named Adolphe Sax. It is made of brass – and so you may think that this instrument should more properly belong to the brass section of the orchestra. But in fact the saxophone makes its sound by means of a single reed and a system of key-work, opening and closing holes cut along the length of its conical tube. Both are characteristics of woodwind instruments rather than brass.

The method of fingering is very similar to that of the clarinet, so that when the saxophone is used in the orchestra, which is fairly rarely, it is played by a clarinettist and so you will find it among the woodwind section on the platform, not the brass.

There is a whole family of saxophones, numbering eight in all, made in a variety of sizes and keys. Those most often used in the orchestra are the E-flat alto and B-flat tenor saxophones, each similar in shape to the bass clarinet.

The single reed and widish bell, and the fact that the saxophone is made of brass, account for its distinctive sound which can be extremely rich and smooth, often with a sweet, haunting tone-quality:

Alto saxophone

Like the clarinet, the saxophone can be very agile, with a wide dynamic range varying from extremely soft to, if necessary, raucously loud – all qualities, of course, which have made the saxophone well suited to playing jazz, especially in the hands of such musicians as Coleman Hawkins, Charlie Parker and Ornette Coleman.

Music to hear

Debussy: Rhapsodie, for saxophone and orchestra
Mussorgsky: 'The Old Castle', from *Pictures at an Exhibition* (orchestrated by Ravel)
Vaughan Williams: 'Dance of Job's Comforters' (three saxophones), from *Job*
Glazounov: Quartet for Saxophones (soprano, alto, tenor, bass)

Bassoon

(I: *fagotto*
F: *basson*
G: *Fagott*)
Size: 2.8 m
Range:

The bassoon is closely related to the oboe. The tube, conical like the oboe's, is so long that it is doubled back upon itself, first downwards, then upwards, with the bell pointing above the player's head. (The Italian and German names for this instrument both mean 'bundle of sticks'.) The double reed of the bassoon, shorter and broader than that of the oboe, is fixed into the end of the metal crook which curves backwards and down to the player's lips. The instrument is supported by a sling, or by a spike resting on the floor in similar fashion to a cello.

Music for bassoon is written in the bass clef, changing to the tenor clef for high notes. It is not a transposing instrument. The tone-quality is rich, reedy, rather dry. Notes in the highest register can sound pinched, somewhat mournful.

The bassoon is a most useful member of the orchestra. It sometimes plays solos. More often it is found supplying the bass-line to the other woodwinds, blending with the horns, or doubling the part played by the cellos to bring an extra 'edge' and vitality to the sound. It is sometimes, unfairly, called the 'clown' of the orchestra. True, played *staccato*, it can chortle with great humour:

But played *legato,* it can sound dignified, if rather sad:

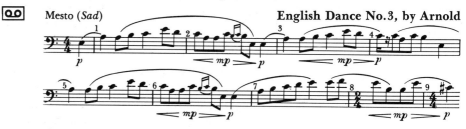

The bassoon joined the orchestra early in the 17th century.

Music to hear

For solo bassoon and orchestra
    Mozart: Bassoon Concerto in B flat major (K191)
    Senaillé: *Allegro Spiritoso*
    Elgar: *Romance,* for bassoon and orchestra

Orchestral solos for bassoon
    Bizet: Prelude to Act 2 ('Les Dragons d'Alcala'), from *Carmen*
    Grieg: 'In the Hall of the Mountain King', from *Peer Gynt*
    Rimsky-Korsakov: second movement from *Scheherazade*
    Stravinsky: opening of *The Rite of Spring* (high register)

Double bassoon

(I: *contrafagotto*
F: *contrebasson*
G: *Kontrafagott*)
Size: 5.6 m
Range:

(sounding)   (written)

The double bassoon, sometimes called the contrabassoon, is pitched an octave lower than the normal bassoon, and plays the deepest notes in the wood-wind section. To make its great length manageable, it is folded into four. Like the bassoon, it has a double reed.

The double bassoon is only included if the orchestra is fairly large. It rarely takes a solo, but is used instead to strengthen the bass-line, providing a solid foundation for the woodwind or giving an 'edge' and definition to the tone of the lower strings. Its music is written one octave higher than it really sounds.

The sound of the double bassoon is deep, dry, and often growling. In 'Beauty and the Beast' from Ravel's *Mother Goose Suite*, it (not surprisingly) represents the Beast. And its sound at the beginning of the same composer's Piano Concerto for the Left Hand has been described as that of a prehistoric monster emerging from a swamp.

Ravel: 'Beauty and the Beast'

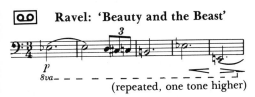

(repeated, one tone higher)

Ravel: Piano Concerto for the Left Hand

Music to hear

The double bassoon is heard grunting in *The Sorcerer's Apprentice* by Dukas (when the two halves of the broken broom begin to stir). It is also heard in the march section of the final movement of Beethoven's 'Choral' Symphony, and in Variation 4 (in duet with a piccolo) from *Variations on a Nursery Song by Dohnányi.*

The woodwind section of the London Phil-harmonic Orchestra Front row: *piccolo, second flute, first flute; first oboe, second oboe, cor anglais.* Back row: *bass clarinet, second clarinet, first clainet; three bassoons.*

Music to hear for woodwind

Composers rarely write for woodwind instruments alone. Most of the pieces mentioned below also include the horn which, though really belonging to the brass section, blends well with woodwind instruments and is also useful in binding the sounds together.

Françaix: Quartet for flute, oboe, clarinet, bassoon
Nielsen: final movement (variations), from Wind Quintet (for flute, oboe interchanging with cor anglais, clarinet, bassoon, horn)
Janáček: *Mladi* (Youth) for wind sextet (flute interchanging with piccolo, oboe, clarinet, bass clarinet, bassoon and horn)
Mozart: Serenade in B flat (K361) for 13 wind instruments (in which the double bassoon part is sometimes taken by double basses)
Dvořák: Serenade in D minor (for wind and low string instruments)

Assignment 14

Identify the instruments from the woodwind section of the orchestra which play the ten extracts recorded on the cassette.

Assignment 15

As you listen to recordings of these pieces, name the instrument from the woodwind section which first plays the tune:

(a) Debussy: *Prélude à l'après-midi d'un faune*
(b) Walton: 'Swiss Yodelling Song', from *Façade*
(c) Grieg: Norwegian Dance No. 2
(d) Rodrigo: slow movement from *Concierto de Aranjuez*
(e) Arnold: English Dance No. 5
(f) Gershwin: *Rhapsody in Blue*
(g) Respighi: 'The Pines of the Appian Way', from *The Pines of Rome*

Assignment 16 Name the two woodwind instruments which are heard playing alternately at the beginning of each of these pieces:

(a) Delius: Intermezzo from *Fennimore and Gerda*
(b) Tchaikovsky: 'Bluebird' Pas de Deux from *The Sleeping Beauty*
(c) Beethoven: Variation 3 from the fourth movement of Septet in E flat
(d) Berlioz: third movement from *Symphonie Fantastique*
(e) Mozart: Trio from the third movement of Symphony No. 39
(f) Dohnányi: Variation 4 from *Variations on a Nursery Song*
(g) Massenet: 'Madrilène', from *Le Cid*
(h) Mussorgsky: 'The Old Castle', from *Pictures at an Exhibition'* (*orchestrated by Ravel*). (Here, a third woodwind instrument briefly joins in.)

A 1. Which instruments in the woodwind section of the orchestra have:
(i) a single reed; (ii) a double reed; (iii) no reed at all?
2. Which woodwind instruments are 'transposing' instruments?
3. What is meant by 'transposing' instruments? Remind yourself of two reasons why their music is written down in such a way.

B Describe the various kinds of clarinet used in the orchestra.
in the orchestra.

C Write out each of the following tunes, correctly transposed, for
(i) clarinet in B flat; (ii) clarinet in A.

(Beethoven: 'Choral' Symphony)

[Key: D major]

(Beethoven: 'Pastoral' Symphony)

[Key: F major]

When you have written out the tunes decide which clarinet, the one in B flat or the one in A, would be most suitable to play each tune.
Give a reason for your answer.

D Explain the similarities, and the differences, between the instruments in each of these pairs:

| clarinet : saxophone | | oboe : bassoon |

E *Research* Find out which woodwind instrument is associated with each of these famous performers:

Anton Stadler	Gwydion Brooke	Heinz Holliger
Leon Goossens	Evelyn Rothwell	Severino Gazzelloni
James Galway	Jack Brymer	Richard Mühlfeld
Benny Goodman	Archie Camden	Frederick the Great

Special assignment A

Each of these pieces features instruments from the strings and the
woodwind sections. Your assignment here is to investigate the ways
in which each composer uses the instruments of these two sections
of the orchestra. As you listen to each piece, carefully follow
the melody-line score and discover the answers to the questions.
Use your eyes and ears to help each other.

1 'Arabian Dance', from the *Nutcracker* Suite   *Tchaikovsky (1840-1893)*

(a) Which woodwind instrument plays the tune at figure **1**?

(b) Name the instrument playing the tune at figure **2**.

(c) Which instruments play the tune at **3**? Which of the Italian
terms in these boxes describes the way they are played?

| pizzicato | con sordino | tremolo |

(d) Which woodwind instrument is playing at **4**?

(e) **4** is repeated, but at a lower pitch. Which instrument plays it
then?

(f) Is the scrap of tune at **5** played by a flute, an oboe, or a
clarinet?

(g) Name the clef used by the bassoon when it plays the final long-
held note, beginning at **6**. Give the alphabetical name of this
particular note.

2 'Berceuse' (Lullaby) from *The Firebird*   *Stravinsky (1882-1971)*

(a) Which instrument doubles the viola notes at figure **1**?

(b) Which instrument plays the tune of the lullaby at figure **2**?

(c) Name the instrument which plays the falling phrases at **3**.

(d) Which instrument takes over the falling phrase at **4**? Is it a cello, bassoon, or saxophone?

(e) Which instruments play the high, soaring melody at **5**?

(f) At **6** and **7,** are the double basses played *pizzicato,* or *arco*?

(g) Which of these terms describes the sounds of the violins at **8**?

pizzicato	harmonics	tremolo	col legno

(h) Describe the way the strings are played at **9**.

(i) At which figure in the melody-line score is the harp heard playing a *glissando*?

4 Brass

The sounds of the brass section, like those of the woodwind, are made by blowing. 'Brass' is a convenient name for these instruments, though nowadays they are more likely to be made from mixed metals than from pure brass. Each instrument is a length of hollow tubing, coiled or folded to make it manageable by the player. A mouth-piece is fixed to one end of the tube; the other end flares into a 'bell'.

The brass section of the modern orchestra often includes:

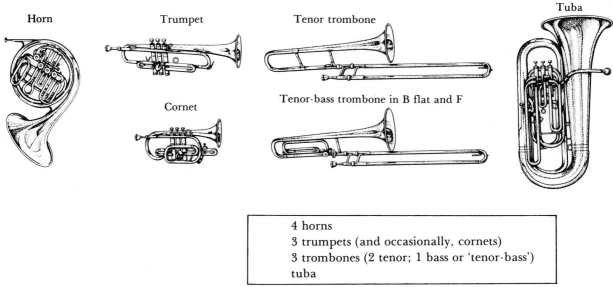

Horn

Trumpet

Cornet

Tenor trombone

Tenor-bass trombone in B flat and F

Tuba

> 4 horns
> 3 trumpets (and occasionally, cornets)
> 3 trombones (2 tenor; 1 bass or 'tenor-bass')
> tuba

These numbers, especially of horns and trumpets, may be increased.

On the concert platform, the brass section is placed behind and above the woodwind and strings:

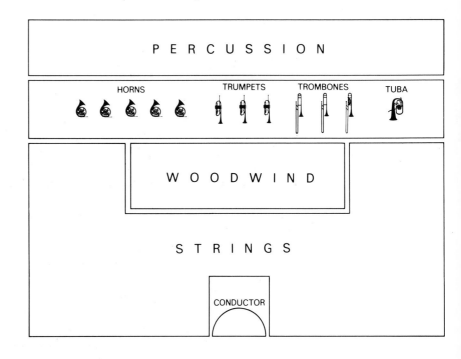

PERCUSSION

HORNS   TRUMPETS   TROMBONES   TUBA

WOODWIND

STRINGS

CONDUCTOR

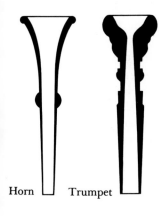

Mouth-pieces

Horn   Trumpet

The tone-quality of a brass instrument depends upon the type of mouthpiece used, the 'bore' (or width) of the tube, and the flare of the bell. The characteristic, brilliant sound of the trumpet, for instance, is due to its narrow, mainly cylindrical bore, the shallow cup-shaped mouth-piece, and the moderately flaring bell. The horn, on the other hand, has a funnel-shaped mouth-piece and the bore gradually expands into a widely flaring bell, giving a rounder, more mellow tone-quality.

Pitch depends upon the length of the tube. The tube of the horn is longer than that of the trumpet, enabling it to sound notes which are lower in pitch.

The player applies his lips to the mouth-piece and, as he blows, makes them vibrate – rather in the same way as the double reed in an oboe or a bassoon. The vibrations of his lips cause the air column inside the instrument also to vibrate, and so a note is sounded. The slacker a player makes his lips, the more slowly they vibrate. This causes the air inside the instrument to vibrate slowly, and so produce a low-pitched note. But the tighter the player's lips, the faster they vibrate, compressing the air inside the instrument so that the vibrations are quicker, producing a note of higher pitch.

The 'harmonic series'

Any tube when blown will, by changing the tension of the lips (tightening or slackening them), produce a certain series of notes. We call these notes the *harmonic series.* The lowest note of the series is called the *fundamental,* and the pitch of this note depends upon the length of the tube. If a tube is of such a length that the fundamental is low C, then a brass-player, by gradually tightening his lips, could sound these notes:

(higher notes are possible, though difficult to produce)

1 2 3 4 5 6 7 8 9 10 11 12 13 14 15 16

(fundamental)

But there are several limitations to all this. On instruments of narrow bore, the fundamental is usually impossible to produce. And there are many gaps in the series – those early on are particularly wide. None of the pitches falling within these gaps can be sounded from that particular length of tube. Only the higher notes of the harmonic series fall close enough together to make any kind of tune possible – and even then, the black notes shown at 7, 11, 13 and 14 sound out of tune.

Of course, a different length of tube would give a new fundamental note (higher if the tube were shorter, lower if it were longer) and then a whole new harmonic series would be offered. But the notes would still be in exactly the same proportion to each other – the second note an octave above the first, the third note at an interval of a fifth above the second, and so on. The gaps, together with the restriction of notes available, would remain precisely the same.

43

These were some of the difficulties faced by early trumpeters and horn-players. In time, several attempts were made to overcome them. The main problem was limitation of available notes. To obtain more notes meant changing the tube-length of the instrument. Of course, trombone-players had always been able to do just that, lengthening or shortening the instrument's tube-length by adjusting the slide.

Crooks

Horn and trumpet players, however, needed a set of 'crooks' – extra lengths of tubing – any of which could be fixed into the instrument temporarily to increase the overall length of the tube. But each crook provided only those notes available from the harmonic series of the new total length of the tube. And a certain amount of time was needed to change crooks.

Early 19th century horn, with crooks

Horn-players found that a few extra notes could be produced by placing the hand inside the bell of the instrument, but the tone of these 'faked' notes was noticeably different from other notes.

In an attempt to increase the range of the trumpet, a type was introduced in 1795 which had side-holes and keys. Unfortunately, boring the holes into the tube robbed the tone of much of its usual brilliance, and so the instrument was found unacceptable. A more successful idea was the invention of a slide mechanism similar to that of the trombone. But although this provided notes to fill the gaps in the harmonic series, the trumpet then became far less agile.

Valves

These problems were finally solved around 1815 by the invention of the valve system. This is the same as having a whole set of crooks permanently fixed into the instrument, any one of which may be instantly selected by the touch of a finger. Each of the three valves brings in an extra length of tubing. When a valve is pressed down the air is diverted along the extra loop (as shown in the simplified drawings of the trumpet below). Valves may be used singly, or in combination, offering a choice of seven fundamental notes, each with its own harmonic series. (The length of tubing at valve 3 is the same as the combined lengths of valves 1 and 2, so that pressing down valve 3 has the same effect as pressing down valves 1 and 2 together.) The player uses the valves as necessary and, by tensing his lips accordingly, selects the required note from the harmonic series offered. The notes possible from all seven harmonic series overlap, so making the trumpet and horn fully chromatic (meaning able to play all semitones) throughout their ranges.

A
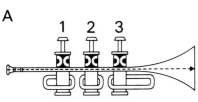

B
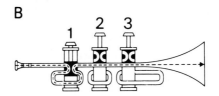

C
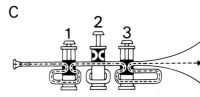

It is important to realise that the main difference between the instruments of the brass section and those belonging to the woodwind is not the material of which they are made, but the way in which they produce their sounds. Instruments belonging to the woodwind section have holes bored along the length of their tubes and their sounds are made by vibrating reeds or, as in the case of the flute and piccolo, by 'edge-tone'. Each instrument in the brass section produces its sounds by means of the player's lips vibrating, at varying degrees of tension, against a metal mouth-piece.

Music to hear

A The three brass variations from *The Young Person's Guide to the Orchestra*, by Benjamin Britten:

1 **Horns** – a sequence of calls, ranging from mysteriously soft to menacingly loud, against a background of violas and cellos, ripples from the harp, and quiet rolls on a kettle drum

2 **Trumpets** – playing strictly in turn in a furious gallop, crisply accompanied by strings and snare drum

3 **Trombones and tuba** – the trombones entering solemnly and very majestically; the tuba pompously, and rather late

B Mussorgsky: 'Catacombs', from *Pictures at an Exhibition* (orchestrated by Ravel)

Quietly supported by low woodwind, the brass section – made up here of 4 horns, 3 trumpets, 3 trombones and tuba – paints an eerie, at times terrifying, impression of someone exploring by lamplight the ancient underground burial chambers which lie beneath the city of Paris. In the middle of this piece, there is a short trumpet solo.

Project file

A Draw a diagram to show how the instruments of the brass section are arranged on the concert platform. Why are they given this position?

B Write down how a player might cause different notes to sound on a brass instrument by using his lips alone.

C Describe these attempts to increase the range of notes of the horn and the trumpet:

crooks	the keyed trumpet	the slide trumpet

Suggest why none of these was, in fact, totally successful.

D Make a note of the advantages offered to trumpet- and horn-players by the invention of the valve system.

Horn

(I: *corno*
F: *cor*
G: *Horn)*
Length of tubing,
about 3.75 m
Range:

(sounding)   (written)

18th century hunting horn

The main ancestor of the modern horn was simply a length of tubing, wound around the shoulder and ending in a flared bell, used to attract attention and give calls and signals during the hunt. It was a horn very like this which was the first kind to be used in the orchestra, towards the end of the 17th century.

The modern orchestral horn-player uses his left hand to control the three valves, supporting the instrument by lightly resting his right hand inside the bell. The valves are usually of the type known as 'rotary' in which, by pressing a lever, the path leading the air into the extra length of tube revolves into position – rather than being lowered, as in the case of the 'piston' valves of the trumpet.

The horn is a transposing instrument, usually pitched in F so that its music is written five notes higher than the real sounds. The tone-quality varies according to how it is played. In smooth, quiet melodies the tone is round and mellow, warm, and rather dark:

Tchaikovsky: Symphony No. 5

But the horn can be played quite forcefully, so that the tone then becomes more rousing – much brighter, and with crisp attack:

Sometimes a horn-player is asked to play 'stopped' notes. To do this, he pushes his hand more firmly inside the bell, causing the sound to become quieter, but thinner and more metallic in quality:

Rimsky-Korsakov: *Spanish Caprice*

(open notes) (stopped notes)

The word *cuivré* (French for 'brassy') instructs the player to wedge his hand very tightly inside the bell, and blow with considerable force. And then the sound becomes very brassy indeed.

A composer may write *'con sordino'* below the music. The player then fixes a pear-shaped mute of metal, wood or cardboard into the bell. This makes the tone thinner, muffled, as if coming from a distance.

Horn-players often now use the 'double-horn', which is really two horns in one. Three rotary valves control two separate sets of valve tubes – one set built on the fundamental note of F; the other, a fourth higher, on B flat. The player can switch from one to the other by means of a fourth valve, worked by the thumb. When set in F, the double horn sounds rich and warm. By switching to B flat, the player can obtain a rather brighter-sounding tone.

Most pieces call for four horns, yet you will often see five players on the platform. The first horn-player is given many tiring solos to play, and so the fifth player (called the 'bumper') gives him time to rest by playing some of his less important passages.

The horn – sometimes not quite correctly called the French horn – is considered one of the most difficult of all instruments to play.

Double horn in F and B flat

Music to hear

For unaccompanied horns
Tippett: Sonata for Four Horns

For solo horn and orchestra
Concertos by Mozart, Richard Strauss, and Hindemith (second movement)

For horn and ensemble
Mozart: Quintet (K407) for horn, violin, 2 violas and cello
Brahms: Scherzo, from Trio in E flat for horn, violin and piano

Orchestral solos
Mendelssohn: Nocturne, from *A Midsummer Night's Dream*
Sibelius: Intermezzo, from *Karelia* Suite (open, then stopped notes)
Beethoven: Trio, from the 'Eroica' Symphony (3 'natural' horns)
Rimsky-Korsakov: Variazioni (theme) from *Spanish Caprice* (4 horns)
Britten: Serenade, for tenor voice, horn, and strings

Trumpet

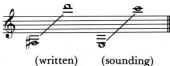

(I: *tromba*
F: *trompette*
G: *Trompete*)
Length of tubing:
1.37 m
Range (trumpet):

(written)　(sounding)

Of the instruments in the brass section, the trumpet is the most ancient. When the tomb of the Egyptian Pharoah Tutankhamun was opened in 1923, two straight trumpets were found – one of silver, the other of copper – dating back to about 1350 B.C.

In medieval times, trumpets were used for military and ceremonial occasions, playing brilliant fanfares based upon the limited notes from the harmonic series (see page 43).

Soon after 1600, the trumpet (now folded into an oblong shape) joined the orchestra, first being used mainly in operas and church music to reinforce passages expressing moods such as joy or triumph.

By the end of the 17th century, trumpeters were developing the difficult skill of playing in the high *clarino* register where notes of the harmonic series fall closely together. This made tunes possible rather than mere fanfares.

oannes a duetecum Lucas duetecum. Fecit.

But by the time of Mozart and Beethoven, the art of clarino-playing had almost died out. Composers were again limited in the range of notes they could write for 'natural' trumpet – the trumpet which, before valves were invented, was restricted to the 'natural' notes of the harmonic series. Crooks (extra lengths of tubing) were used to change the overall pitch, but the notes available were still limited to the harmonic series of the new total length of the tube.

The following typical fanfare is from Beethoven's opera *Fidelio*, announcing the arrival of the prison governor to save the wrongfully imprisoned Florestan from death. It is first heard off-stage and then from the orchestra pit, as if drawing nearer:

Several attempts were made to increase the possible range of notes (such as the introduction of the keyed trumpet and the slide trumpet described on page 46) but it was not until the invention of valves around the year 1815 that the problem was successfully solved. The valve system now enables the modern trumpet to rival woodwind instruments in both range of notes and agility:

Tchaikovsky: Neapolitan Dance from *Swan Lake*

Andante flessibile
(trumpet in B flat)

mp espressivo

Allegro brillante

f con brio

When necessary, the trumpet's brilliant and penetrating tone-quality can ring out thrillingly above the entire orchestra.

Various kinds of mute can be used to change the tone-quality, or for special effects. When played quietly, a 'straight' mute softens the tone and gives an effect of coming mysteriously from the distance. But if blown forcefully, the tone can become harsh and sinister. Other kinds of mute – used particularly in jazz and 'pop' music – include cup, plunger and wowwow.

Mutes

wowwow plunger straight cup

The trumpet most often used in the orchestra is pitched in B flat (with music, like that of the clarinet in B flat, written one tone higher than it actually sounds). But trumpets in C are also common, and for pieces written in the high clarino register by composers such as Bach, smaller trumpets pitched in C, D and high F are used.

Music to hear

For unaccompanied trumpets
    Britten: *Fanfare for St Edmundsbury,* for three trumpets (three separate solo fanfares, later played simultaneously)

For solo trumpet and orchestra
    Bach: Brandenburg Concerto No. 2 (high *clarino* register)
    Purcell: Trumpet Tune and Air; Sonata in D for trumpet and strings
    Concertos by Haydn (for keyed trumpet), and Hummel

Orchestral solos for trumpet
    Verdi: 'Grand March', from the opera *Aida*
    Shostakovich: Piano Concerto No. 1 (middle of the fourth movement)
    Panufnik: 'Vision 1', from *Sinfonia Sacra* (four trumpets positioned at the four 'corners' of the orchestra)
    Mussorgsky: 'Samuel Goldenberg and Schmuyle', from *Pictures at an Exhibition,* orchestrated by Ravel (muted trumpets)

The trumpet in jazz
    Recordings featuring Louis Armstrong, Dizzy Gillespie, Miles Davis

Cornet

(I: *cornetto*
F: *cornet à pistons*
G: *Kornett*)
(Size and range the same as the trumpet in B flat)

The cornet is a descendant of the posthorn – the long brass instrument which announced the arrival of the mail coach at a town or village. The cornet was invented in France around 1825. It is squarer in shape than the trumpet. The bore is mainly conical and the mouth-piece is funnel-shaped. The tone is less brilliant than the trumpet, less mellow than the horn. Cornets are 'extras' in the brass section and are used only in certain pieces.

Allegro fastoso   **Prokofiev:** *Lieutenant Kijé*

(sounding one tone lower)

Music to hear   Stravinsky: 'Royal March', from *The Soldier's Tale*

Trombone

(I: *trombone*
F: *trombone*
G: *Posaune*)
Size (with the slide in): 2.75 m
Range (tenor trombone):

The Italian name means 'big trumpet', and the trombone is in fact a long, folded trumpet with a more deeply cupped mouth-piece. In its medieval form it was called *sackbut* – from an Old French word *sacqueboute* (meaning 'pull-push'). The instrument has changed surprisingly little since that time.

These low notes (called 'pedal' notes) are also possible:

Instead of valves, the trombone has a movable slide – a U-shaped length of tubing which telescopes into the main tube. The player can easily and immediately adjust this slide to lengthen or shorten the total length of the tube. Because of this, the trombone has never been bothered by the problem of gaps in the harmonic series. There are seven positions for the slide, based on seven fundamental notes. The player selects notes from the various harmonic series offered by these fundamentals by varying the tension of his lips.

The trombone can sound solemn, noble and dignified:

Mozart: Tuba mirum, from Requiem in D minor

Played forcefully, the tone blazes with an exciting, aggressive sound which can easily dominate the rest of the orchestra:

Rimsky-Korsakov: *Scheherazade*

But the trombone can be played in lighter style, sometimes including the *glissando*, in which the player continues to blow as he moves the slide – literally sliding from one note to another:

Copland: *Rodeo*

The trombone can be muted in the same way as the trumpet, bringing a rather sinister quality to the tone but with a crisp attack.

There are usually three trombones in a large orchestra: two tenor and one bass, or 'tenor-bass'. The true bass trombone is pitched a fourth below the tenor but due to its greater length the slide is not easy to manage. It is usually replaced now by the tenor-bass trombone. This is the same size as the tenor, but with the bore of the bass. There is an extra length of tubing brought in when needed by a thumb-lever, lowering the pitch to that of the bass trombone. Sometimes an alto trombone (pitched a fourth higher than the tenor) and double bass trombone (a fifth lower than the bass) are included.

Trombones are not transposing instruments.

Tuba

(I: *tuba*
F: *tuba*
G: *Tuba*)
Tube length (bass
tuba): 3.65 m
Range:

('Pedal notes')

The tuba plays the lowest notes in the brass section. It is the youngest member of the section, having been invented during the 1820s.

Tubas are made in several sizes and pitches, and have from three to five valves. Those most often used in the modern orchestra are the tenor tuba (or euphonium) in B flat, and the bass tuba in F. But many players now use the 'double tuba' which, like the double horn and the tenor-bass trombone, combines two pitches within the same instrument.

The wide conical bore and cup-shaped mouth-piece give the tuba a tone-quality which is round and full, rich, but rather 'tubby'. It is sometimes given a melody:

Wagner: Overture to *The Mastersingers*

Molto moderato

More often, however, the tuba reinforces the bass-line of the music and provides a solid foundation for the brass section. Occasionally, it is heard playing distinctive 'oom-pahs'.

Like the other brass, the tuba is sometimes muted. The mute is a huge cone, usually of cardboard, more than 60 cm high.

Music to hear

Vaughan Williams: Concerto for Tuba and Orchestra
Mussorgsky: 'Bydlo' (The Ox-cart), from *Pictures at an Exhibition* (orchestrated by Ravel)
Tchaikovsky: finale from the 'Pathétique' Symphony (fairly near the end, underlining the solemn passage for three trombones)

The brass section of the London Philharmonic Orchestra
From the left: five horns (including the 'bumper'); four trumpets;
two tenor trombones and tenor-bass trombone; bass tuba

Music to hear for brass

Dukas: 'Fanfare' from *La Péri,* for the normal orchestral brass section
Poulenc: Allegro, from Sonata for horn, trombone and trumpet
Arnold: Con brio, from Brass Quintet for 2 trumpets, horn, trombone and tuba
Dodgson: Poco adagio, from Sonata for Brass (muted brass sounds)
Renaissance pieces by Susato and Giovanno Gabrieli played on modern brass (then compare with performances on original instruments)
Locke: *Music for His Majesty's Sackbuts and Cornetts* (composed for the Coronation of King Charles II)
Bliss: *Antiphonal Fanfare* for three brass choirs (composed by a former Master of the Queen's Musick for the Investiture of His Royal Highness, the Prince of Wales)
(All the pieces listed above are grouped together on the Decca record SPA 464: 'The World of Brass')

53

Assignment 17 Identify the instruments from the brass section of the orchestra which play the twelve extracts recorded on the cassette.

Assignment 18 As you listen to recordings of each of the following pieces, name the brass instrument which first plays a solo:

(a) Richard Strauss: *Till Eulenspiegel*
(b) Mussorgsky: 'Bydlo' (The Ox-cart), from *Pictures at an Exhibition* (orchestrated by Ravel)
(c) Holst: *The Perfect Fool*
(d) Bizet: 'La Garde Montante', from the opera *Carmen*
(e) Ravel: *Pavane for a Dead Princess*
(f) Rimsky-Korsakov: Suite from the opera *The Golden Cockerel*

Assignment 19 Each of these pieces begins with two or more brass instruments of the same kind. Which instruments are they?

(a) Dvořák: final movement of Symphony No. 8 in G major
(b) Schumann: fourth movement from Symphony No. 3 ('Rhenish')
(c) Beethoven: Trio, from the third movement of the 'Eroica' Symphony
(d) Tchaikovsky: Variation 3 ('Miettes qui tombent') of the Pas de Six from Act 1 of the ballet *The Sleeping Beauty*
(e) Delibes: Prelude to the ballet *Coppélia*
(f) Delibes: 'The Procession of Bacchus', from the ballet *Sylvia*

Assignment 20 At the beginning of each of these pieces one kind of brass instrument is soon followed, or joined, by another. Name both kinds.

(a) Handel: Allegro deciso, from *The Water Music*
(b) Wagner: Overture to the opera *The Flying Dutchman*
(c) Stravinsky: 'Royal March', from *The Soldier's Tale*
(d) Rossini: 'Gallop', from the Overture to the opera *William Tell*

Assignment 21 Look carefully at the fanfare for a 'natural' trumpet on page 48. Compare the notes of this fanfare with those of the harmonic series based on the fundamental note of C on page 43. Which numbered notes of the harmonic series does this fanfare use?

Assignment 22 Examine the snatches of music below. In each case explain what the player would do to reproduce the music, and then describe the kind of sounds the instrument would make.

54

Project file

A 1. What are the main differences between the instruments of the brass section and those belonging to the woodwind section?
   2. Note three reasons which account for the particular tone-quality of a brass instrument.

B 1. Write down some ways in which a horn-player might alter the tone-quality of the sound of his instrument.
   2. What is meant by a 'double horn'?

C 1. What is the difference in tone-quality between a trumpet and a cornet?
   2. If you listened to a muted trumpet played (i) *pianissimo,* and (ii) *fortissimo* what difference in tone-quality and effect would you hear?

D Until the 19th century, crooks were used on trumpets and horns. Why were they unnecessary as far as the trombone was concerned?

E 1. Write down – and remind yourself, perhaps, with a drawing – how the player makes the different notes on a trombone.
   2. What is meant by a 'tenor-bass' trombone?

F 1. When was the tuba invented?
   2. What is meant by a 'double tuba'?
   3. Write down two things which make the tone-quality of the tuba sound rich and rather fat.

G Write out each of these snatches of music for:
   (i) trumpet in B flat
   (ii) horn in F
   (iii) an octave lower, in the tenor clef, for trombone

(a)

(b)

H *Research* Find out which brass instrument is associated with each of these well-known performers:

Dennis Brain	'Punto'	Alan Civil
Philip Jones	Dizzie Gillespie	John Wilbraham
'Satchmo'	Barry Tuckwell	Tommy Dorsey
Michael Hext	John Fletcher	Bix Beiderbecke

Special assignment B

'The Battle and Defeat of Napoleon'   *Kodály (1882-1967)*

This comes from a suite of pieces drawn from the music which Kodály composed to accompany a play about a Hungarian soldier, Háry János, who is famous for telling wildly exaggerated stories about his brave exploits and adventures. This piece describes how he conquered the entire French Army and brought its great General, Napoleon, quaking to his knees.

Here are the four main tunes:

Listen to this piece, answering these questions:

(a) Which instruments from the brass section of the orchestra play Tune A?

(b) This tune is immediately repeated. Which instruments play it then?

(c) Which instrument plays the distant echo of the fanfare (Tune B)?

(d) Tune A is heard again, and then repeated as before:
  (i) Describe the sounds made by the trumpets when it is repeated.
  (ii) Which Italian words would be written beneath their music here?

(e) Below the trills played by the trumpets 8 bars later, the Italian phrase *senza sordino* is written. What does this mean?

(f) Two different kinds of brass instrument play the low notes of Tune C. Name both kinds.

(g) (i) Which instrument plays the tune of the grotesque funeral march which ends this piece (Tune D)?
  (ii) To which section of the orchestra does this instrument properly belong? Give a reason for your answer.

(h) In which of these four tunes are the trombones heard playing glissandos?

(i) Do you think Tune D is similar in any way to Tune A – or does Kodály bring in a completely new tune here?

(j) Which main member of the brass section of the orchestra is *not* heard in this piece?

Special assignment C

Prelude to the opera *Irmelin*   *Delius (1862-1934)*

Listen to this Prelude, carefully following the melody-line score.

(a) Which woodwind instrument plays the first phrase (figure **1**)?

(b) At figure **2** do you hear a piccolo, a clarinet, or a bassoon?

(c) Which instrument plays the solo phrase at figure **3**?

(d) Which instruments take the melody at figure **4**?

(e) Is **5** played by horns, violas, or double basses?

(f) Is **6** played by a bassoon, a double bassoon, or a bass clarinet?

(g) Which instrument plays the single bar at figure **7**?

(h) Which instrument plays in octaves at figure **8**?

(i) Is **9** played by a piccolo, a flute, or a clarinet?

(j) **10, 11** and **12** are played by oboe, cor anglais, and clarinet – but in which order are these three instruments heard here?

(k) Which Italian phrase would be written below the violin notes at figure **13** to produce these hushed, silvery sounds?

(l) Which two solo woodwind instruments play at **14** and **15**?

(m) Which instrument plays the repeated phrase at figure **16**?

(n) Which two solo string instruments play at **17** and **18**?

(o) Which instrument plays the final phrase, at figure **19**?

5
Percussion

14th-century percussion player

Percussion instruments are those which are struck or shaken. Some of these are the oldest of all instruments, reaching back to the dawn of human history when they were used for dancing, rituals, sending signals and making war. But even so, the percussion is the most recent section of the orchestra to become really established.

Percussion instruments can be divided into two groups. The first group contains 'tuned' percussion instruments – those able to play one or more notes of definite pitch, and could therefore possibly play a tune. These include:

kettle drums (or timpani)	celesta
glockenspiel	vibraphone
xylophone	tubular bells

The second group is larger, and includes all 'non-tuned' percussion instruments. These produce sounds of indefinite pitch and can play only rhythms, not tunes. However colourful and exciting these instruments may sound, they must really be called 'noise-makers':

bass drum	triangle	tam-tam (or gong)
snare drum (or side drum)	tambourine	whip
tenor drum	castanets	sleighbells
cymbals	woodblocks	maracas

As the percussion section is quite likely to make the most noise, it is positioned up at the back of the concert platform:

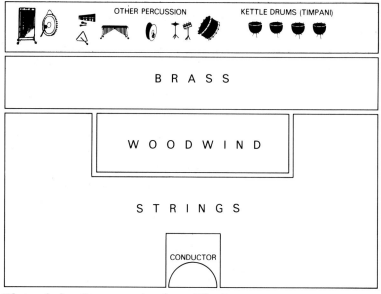

Music to hear

The variation for percussion from *The Young Person's Guide to the Orchestra,* by Benjamin Britten:

1	**kettle drums**	5	**xylophone**
2	**bass drum and cymbals**	6	**castanets and tam-tam**
3	**tambourine and triangle**	7	**whip**
4	**snare drum and woodblock**		

Timpani, *or kettle drums*

(I: *timpani*
F: *timbales*
G: *Pauken*)
Diameters and ranges:

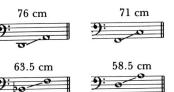

76 cm   71 cm

63.5 cm   58.5 cm

The kettle drum is the only drum in the orchestra which produces a note of definite pitch. The drumhead, of calfskin or plastic, is stretched over a copper bowl. Tension on the skin is adjusted by turning T-shaped screws around the rim. Tightening the skin raises the pitch; slackening it lowers the pitch. Pedal-tuned (or 'chromatic') kettle drums are now often used in which the pitch can be quickly changed by a footpedal, instead of by hand. Modern composers occasionally ask for the pitch to be changed while a drum is actually being played.

The timpanist may play single strokes, or a 'roll' by using left and right sticks alternately and very swiftly; or he may play complicated rhythms on as many as four kettle drums in combination. The sticks may be headed with felt, sponge, cork or wood. Softness or hardness of the heads affects attack, volume and tone-quality.

Timpanists play kettle drums only – leaving other players to manage any other percussion instruments called for in the music.

Kettle drums found a place in the orchestra in the 17th century. For a considerable while, they were the only percussion instruments.

Pedal-tuned
kettle drum

Sibelius: Scherzo from Symphony No. 1 in E minor
Nielsen: Finale from Symphony No. 4 (Two sets of kettle drums)
Berlioz: 'Tuba mirum' from the Requiem (10 players – 16 kettle drums!)
Bartók: Third movement from *Music for Strings, Percussion and Celesta* (pedal-tuned kettle drums)

Bass drum

(I: *gran cassa*
F: *grosse caisse*
G: *grosse Trommel*)
Diameter: 76 cm

The bass drum may have two drumheads, or one only. The screwheads are adjusted to give the best resonance – but this drum does not produce a note of definite pitch, merely a low-pitched 'boom'. It has more carrying power than any other instrument in the orchestra. Played softly, the sound is 'felt' rather than heard. Played loudly, it can be electrifying. The bass drumstick has a large, fairly soft head. Single strokes may be made, or a roll played with kettle drum sticks. Special effects include strokes with hard sticks, wire brushes, or a bundle of birch rods.

Rossini: 'Storm' section from the Overture to *William Tell*
Berlioz: fourth and fifth movements from *Symphonie Fantastique*

Snare drum, or side drum

(I: *tamburo militare*
or *tamburo piccolo*
F: *tambour militaire*
or *caisse claire*
G: *kleine Trommel*)
Diameter: 38 cm

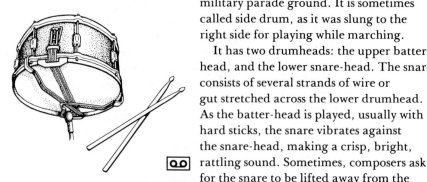

This drum came to the orchestra from the military parade ground. It is sometimes called side drum, as it was slung to the right side for playing while marching.

It has two drumheads: the upper batter-head, and the lower snare-head. The snare consists of several strands of wire or gut stretched across the lower drumhead. As the batter-head is played, usually with hard sticks, the snare vibrates against the snare-head, making a crisp, bright, 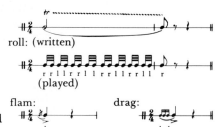 rattling sound. Sometimes, composers ask for the snare to be lifted away from the drumhead, so only the two skins vibrate.

Snare drum strokes include the roll, the flam, and the drag. The roll is played by rapidly alternating double strokes with each stick – two with the right, then two with the left, and so on. The flam is an accented note preceded by a single grace-note. The drag is an accented note preceded by two, or more, grace-notes.

roll: (written)

r r l l r r l l r r l l r r l l   r
(played)

flam: drag:
r l   l r l r

Special effects include: using wire brushes; the 'rim-shot', made by placing the left stick with the tip on the drumhead, the middle of the stick touching the rim, then striking the left stick sharply with the right, producing a noise like a gun-shot; and playing 'on the rim' – using the sticks on the wooden or metal rim of the drum instead of (or as well as) the skin.

The tenor drum is really a deeper side drum but with no snare.

Khachaturian: 'Lezghinka', a barbaric dance from the ballet *Gayaneh*
Nielsen: first movement from Symphony No. 5 (at the climax of which the composer instructs the snare drum player to improvise freely 'as if at all costs to stop the progress of the music')

Cymbals

(I: *piatti*
F: *cymbales*
G: *Becken*)
Diameter: up to 46 cm

Cymbals are dishes of metal alloy. A pair of cymbals may be clashed and allowed to ring on, or be suddenly damped by bringing the edges smartly to the player's chest. Two cymbals may be gently brushed together; or agitated to produce a 'two-plate roll'.

A suspended cymbal may be struck in various ways: with a hard or soft drumstick; wire brush; metal triangle beater; even a penknife blade. A cymbal roll may add great excitement to an orchestral *crescendo*. You may sometimes see two cymbals fixed one above the other on a stand, worked by a foot-pedal. This is called a hi-hat.

Dvořák: *Slavonic Dances* Nos. 1 and 8 (cymbals clashed, *ff*)
Bartók: slow movement of Sonata for two pianos and percussion (*pp*)

Glockenspiel

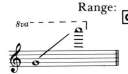

(I: *campanelli*
F: *carillon*
G: *Glockenspiel*)
Range:

The glockenspiel has 30 oblong plates of steel, grade in length and arranged like a piano keyboard. The player uses light mallets with heads of hard or soft rubber, wood or metal. The tone is bright and silvery (this German word means 'play of bells').

Tchaikovsky: 'Chinese Dance', from the *Nutcracker* Suite

Xylophone

Range:

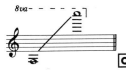

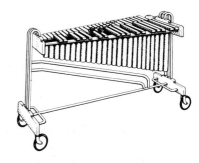

The xylophone is similar to the glockenspiel except the bars are of hard wood instead of metal (this is a Greek word meaning 'sounds from wood'). Resonators beneath the bars help to enrich and sustain the sound. The tone is hard and very bright, though soft-headed mallets can be used.

Saint-Saëns: 'Fossils', from *The Carnival of Animals*

Celesta

Range:

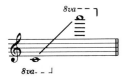

This is really a glockenspiel with a keyboard like a small piano. As keys are pressed down, tiny hammers strike steel bars. Each bar has a wooden resonator which makes the tone silvery, delicate and chiming.

Holst: 'Neptune, the Mystic' (quarter-way through) from *The Planets*

Vibraphone

Range:

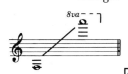

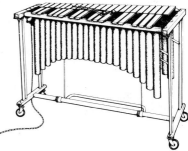

This is another instrument similar to the glockenspiel. Hand-held mallets strike steel slabs below which are resonating tubes, each tuned to the note above. At the top of each resonator is a fan, revolved by electricity, which makes the sound pulsate with a rich, sweet tone.

Shchedrin: 'Habañera' (half-way through) from *The Carmen Ballet*

Triangle

(I: *triangolo*
F: *triangle*
G: *Triangel*)

Triangles are narrow bars of rounded steel bent into triangular shape with one corner left open. They are made in various sizes. A triangle is suspended and struck with a metal beater: either with single 'tings'; or with a 'trill' – rattling the beater in the upper corner. The sound is very penetrating – high, but with no definite pitch.

Borodin: 'Tartars' Dance', from the *Polovtsian Dances*
Liszt: Scherzando, from the second movement of Piano Concerto No. 1
    (the triangle part is almost as difficult as the solo piano part!)

Tambourine

(I: *tamburo basco*
F: *tambour de basque*
G: *Schellentrommel*)

The tambourine is a small, single-headed drum with pairs of thin brass discs set into slots around the rim. It may be shaken, so that only the 'jingles' sound; or the drumhead struck with fingertips, knuckles, fist, back of the hand, or against the knee. The tip of the thumb, moistened, may be run across the skin so that friction makes it rebound, causing both drumhead and jingles to sound. The tambourine may be set down head uppermost and played with drumsticks.

Malcolm Arnold: English Dance No. 8

Castanets

(I: *castagnette*
F: *castagnettes*
G: *Kastagnetten*)

These originated in Spain and are often used to bring a Spanish flavour to a piece of music. The true Spanish castanets are separate tiny saucers of hard wood (*castaña* – Spanish for 'chestnut'). These are joined by a string, wound around thumb and finger, and clicked together with great rhythmic precision. But orchestral castanets, for convenience, are usually hinged on a stick and either shaken or tapped one against the other, by the hand or on the knee.

Tchaikovsky: 'Spanish Dance', from *Swan Lake* (followed by tambourine)

Woodblocks

The woodblock is quite simply a block of wood with a slot hollowed through making a resonating cavity. It is played with snare drum sticks or xylophone mallets. The Chinese block gives a hollow tapping sound of indefinite pitch. Temple blocks, of varying sizes, produce hollow-sounding notes of definite pitch.

Copland: 'Hoe-Down', from *Rodeo* (Chinese block)
Shchedrin: First Intermezzo from *The Carmen Ballet* (temple blocks)

Tubular bells

(I: *campane*
F: *cloches*
G: *Glocken)*
Range:

The bells used in the orchestra are hollow steel tubes, graded in length to give different pitches. The player strikes them near the top with a wooden mallet. Composers use their sounds for dramatic, colourful effects, especially to give the impression of church bells.

Tchaikovsky: *1812 Overture*

Tam-tam, or gong

Diameter: up to 1.5 m

The tam-tam, originating from the Far East, is a huge bronze gong. The rim is bent over so that the edge does not vibrate. Strokes or rolls played softly sound mysterious. Aggressive strokes or a roll played *crescendo* are most dramatic, even terrifying. The beater is usually soft and covered with chamois, but other sticks can be used for special effects.

Cui: *Orientale*

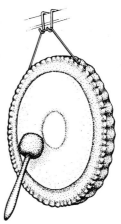

Other percussion instruments

The number and variety of instruments which may appear in the percussion section are actually without limit. Others you may hear include: the whip – two hinged pieces of wood slapped smartly together; sleighbells; maracas – dried gourds inside which the seeds rattle when shaken; guiro – a large gourd with notches, scraped with a stick; claves – sticks clicked together; and rattle – similar to the football variety! Also, of course, piano. And various other kinds of drum, such as bongos or tom-toms.

Composers may even ask for special 'colour' effects from cowbells, anvils, chains, motor-car horns, sirens, whistles, wind machine, or breaking glass.

The percussion section of the London Philharmonic Orchestra

Music to hear for percussion

Daniel Jones: Sonata for four timpani
Stockhausen: *Zyklus* (for one percussionist playing snare drum, wood drums, cymbals, triangle, tam-tam, tom-toms, guiro, suspended bunch of bells, cowbells, vibraphone, and marimba – a large mellow-toned xylophone with tuned metal tubular resonators)
Varèse: *Ionisation* (for 42 percussion instruments and two sirens, managed by 13 players)
Bartók: Sonata for two pianos and percussion (3 kettle drums, xylophone, 2 snare drums – one with snare, the other with snare lifted – suspended cymbal, pair of cymbals, bass drum, triangle, tam-tam)
Stockhausen: *Kontakte* (for percussionist playing a great variety of percussion instruments, and pianist who must play several percussion instruments in addition to the piano)
Shchedrin: *The Carmen Ballet* (for string section and 47 percussion instruments managed by 5 players)
Carl Orff: 'Ecce gratum', 'Floret silva', and 'Veni, veni, venias', from *Carmina Burana*

Assignment 23

Identify the percussion instruments which play the fifteen extracts recorded on the cassette.

Assignment 24

As you listen to the beginning of each of these pieces, name the first percussion instrument you hear:
(a) Bizet: 'Marche', from *Jeux d'Enfants*
(b) Delius: 'La Calinda', from *Koanga*

(c) Massenet: 'Aubade', from *Le Cid*

(d) Elgar: Variation 7, 'Troyte', from *Enigma Variations*

(e) Walton: 'Noche Espagnole', from *Façade*

(f) Walton: 'Swiss Yodelling Song', from *Façade*

(g) Rossini: Valse Lente, from *La Boutique Fantasque* (arranged by Respighi)

(h) Orff: 'Chramer, gip die varwe mir', from *Carmina Burana*

(i) Orff: 'Fortune plango vulnera', from *Carmina Burana*

(j) Penderecki: Symphony (1973)

(k) Khachaturian: Lullaby, from *Gayaneh*

(l) Tchaikovsky: 'Dance of the Sugar-Plum Fairy', from *The Nutcracker*

(m) Vaughan Williams: first movement from Symphony No. 8

(n) Shostakovich: Polka, from *The Age of Gold*

Assignment 25

Three, or more, percussion instruments are involved at the beginning of each of these pieces:

(a) Dvořák: *Carnival Overture*

(b) Kodály: 'Viennese Musical Clock', from *Háry János*

(c) Villa-Lobos: *The Little Train of the Caipira*

Assignment 26

Listen to each of these pieces complete. As you listen to each one, note down all the percussion instruments you can identify.

(a) Kodály: 'The Battle and Defeat of Napoleon', from *Háry János* (the tunes for this piece are printed on page 56)

(b) Walton: 'Popular Song', from *Façade*

(c) Arnold: English Dance No. 7

Assignment 27

Listen to these three songs from *Carmina Burana,* by Carl Orff:

(a) 'Veris leta facies'

(b) 'Circa mea pectora'

(c) 'Tempus est jocundum'

As you listen to each song, note down the percussion instruments used in the accompaniment. Afterwards, make three lists and enter each instrument according to the vibrating material which produces its sounds: skin, metal, wood.

Project file

A 1. Describe how the instruments of the percussion section of the orchestra can be divided into two groups.

2. Listen to 'The Entrance of the Emperor and his Court', from Kodály's *Háry János*. Note down the percussion instruments you hear, then afterwards list them according to the two groups you have described.

B Describe the instruments you would expect to find in the percussion section of a large modern orchestra. Include drawings to illustrate your description.

Special assignment D

Each of these pieces features instruments from the four sections of the orchestra in a rather special way. Your assignment here is to investigate the sounds to discover which instruments are being used and, in some cases, the manner in which they are played.

1 'Scena', from *Spanish Caprice*

Rimsky-Korsakov (1844-1908)

Follow the melody-line score as you listen to this music to help you to answer the questions below. (The Italian word *cadenza* means a florid, usually difficult, passage for one or more soloists.)

(a) Which instrument plays the tune of the fanfare at figure 1?

(b) Which percussion instrument accompanies this fanfare? Is it playing a roll, a flam, or a drag?

(c) Which instrument plays the solo *cadenza* at figure **2**? Describe the sounds it produces at the end of this *cadenza*.

(d) Which instrument plays the notes A and E in the two bars at figure **3**? Name two other instruments heard in these two bars, and describe how they are being played.

(e) Describe the way the violins are played at figure **4**.

(f) Which instrument plays a roll at figure **5**?

(g) Name the instrument which plays the *cadenza* at figure **6**.

(h) Which instrument plays the *cadenza* at figure **7**?

(i) Which instrument accompanies at **7**? Describe how it is played.

(j) Name the instrument which plays the tune at figure **8**.

(k) Which instrument accompanies at figure **8**? How is it played?

(l) Name the instrument which plays the *cadenza* at figure **9**. Which Italian word describes the way this *cadenza* ends?

(m) Name two instruments which punch out the chords at figure **10**.

(n) Identify the percussion sounds at figure **10** and describe the way they are played.

2 'Giuoco delle Coppie' (The Game of the Couples), from *Concerto for Orchestra*   Bartók (1881-1945)

Bartók was born in Hungary but eventually went to live in America where this work was written in 1943, shortly before he died. He explained that he gave it the title *Concerto* because there are many occasions in the music when the instruments - either singly, or in groups - are given extremely difficult passages to play.

Giuoco delle Coppie is the second of the five movements. The 'couples' are in fact five pairs of instruments, introduced in turn. As you listen to this music, answer these questions:

(a) First there is a short, rhythmic introduction. Which instrument plays this? What is special about its sound here?

(b) Then we meet the first 'couple'. Which instruments are these? Which Italian word describes the way in which the strings are being played in the background?

(c) Which instruments make up the second couple? What have these instruments in common with the preceding pair?

(d) Which couple appears next? Have these instruments a single, or a double, reed?

(e) Name the next pair of instruments, and briefly describe how they make their sound.

(f) Which instruments make up the final couple? Describe the special sound they make here, and suggest which Italian words would be written below their notes.

(g) The central section of this piece is given mainly to one section of the orchestra. Which section is this? Are these instruments played with or without mutes here? Which instrument plays the rhythmic accompaniment between their solemn phrases?

(h) The couples reappear, but now with other instruments discreetly adding extra strands of colour here and there. Are the couples heard in the same order as before, or is the order rearranged?

7 Full orchestra

The number, and the different kinds, of instruments which make up an orchestra vary enormously from one century to the next, from one work to another – even from movement to movement within the same composition. For one piece, 'full orchestra', may mean twenty or so players. For another, a hundred and twenty or more. Let us take a look at six very different orchestras spanning more than 350 years.

One of the first orchestras we know about in some detail is that used by the Italian composer Monteverdi in 1607 for his opera *Orfeo*. When the music was printed two years later, Monteverdi included this list of instruments which he wanted to take part:

Duoi Gravicembani.	Two harpsichords
Duoi contrabaſſi de Viola.	Two double bass viols (similar to our modern double basses)
Dieci Viole da brazzo.	Group of 10 strings (probably including violins, violas and cellos)
Vn Arpa doppia.	One double harp
Duoi Violini piccoli alla Franceſe.	Two small-sized violins
Duoi Chitaroni.	Two chitarrone (large bass lutes)
Duoi Organi di legno.	Two small organs with wooden pipes
Tre baſſi da gamba.	Three bass viols (roughly similar to our modern cellos)
Quattro Tromboni.	Four trombones
Vn Regale.	One small organ with reed pipes
Duoi Cornetti.	Two cornetts (of wood, with finger-holes, but trumpet-like mouth-piece)
Vn Flautino alla Vigeſima ſeconda.	One tiny, high-sounding recorder
Vn Clarino con tre trombe ſordine.	One *clarino* (high-sounding trumpet) and three 'soft' trumpets.

This seems an odd assortment of instruments, but it is important to realise that at that time there was no accepted standard for what an orchestra should be. Monteverdi asked for this particular 'orchestra' only for *Orfeo*. On another occasion, he would have written for a quite different combination of instruments.

During the 17th century, the perfecting of string instruments, the violin in particular, led to the string section (first and second violins, violas, cellos and double basses) becoming established as a balanced and self-contained unit – a central nucleus to which composers attached other instruments in ones and twos: flutes and oboes (but rarely both in the same piece until the end of the 18th century), bassoons, horns and occasionally trumpets and kettle drums. In addition, a harpsichord or organ was included. This was called the *continuo* – the player 'continuing' throughout the music to fill out the harmonies and decorate the textures.

Bach's Orchestral Suite No. 4 in D major (thought to have been composed around 1720, though possibly 1730) is scored for:

oboes	trumpets
bassoon	kettle drums
strings, and *continuo*	

The movements of the Suite are called: Overture, Bourrées I and II, Gavotte, Menuets I and II, and 'Réjouissance'. Trumpets and drums are silent in Bourrée II and Menuet I; and Bach scores Menuet II for the strings (and *continuo*) only.

Towards the end of the 18th century the woodwind instruments, now joined by the recently invented clarinets, formed themselves into a self-contained orchestral section (the sections of the orchestra in fact became established in the same order as they have been discussed in this book – strings, woodwind, brass, percussion).

Haydn's last Symphony, No. 104 in D major (the 'London'), written in 1795, is scored for:

2 flutes
2 oboes
2 clarinets
2 bassoons
2 horns
2 trumpets
2 kettle drums
strings
(the harpsichord
continuo now falling
out of use)

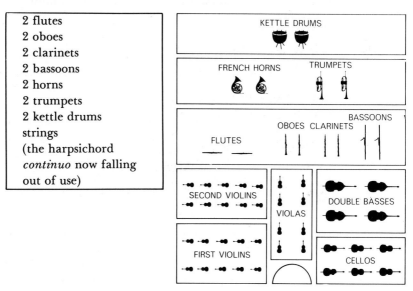

For a while the formation of the orchestra as shown above was standard. Beethoven's first four symphonies, composed at the beginning of the 19th century, employ the same instruments – except for an extra horn in the Third Symphony (the 'Eroica'). In his Fifth Symphony (1807) he included trombones which until then had been used only in operas and church music. But it was not until valves were introduced in about 1815, finally freeing horns and trumpets from the limitations of the harmonic series, that composers really thought of the brass as forming an orchestral section in its own right. However, the greater flexibility offered by the addition of valves, together with improvements in tone and tuning, raised the brass to important status in the orchestra used by the Romantic composers of the 19th century. The number of horns was increased to four, and the tuba was included to provide a bass for the section.

Extra woodwind – piccolo, cor anglais, bass clarinet and double bassoon – were also available. And the kettle drums were now often joined by a selection of other percussion instruments to emphasise the rhythms or provide a dash of colour.

Tchaikovsky – who had a superb gift for orchestration – scored his Fantasy-Overture *Romeo and Juliet,* composed in 1880, for:

2 flutes and piccolo	4 horns	3 kettle drums
2 oboes and cor anglais	2 trumpets	bass drum
2 clarinets	3 trombones	cymbals
2 bassoons	tuba	

and a larger string section (including harp) to balance

At the end of the 19th century and the beginning of the 20th, the orchestra was, on occasion, vastly expanded, especially in the symphonies of Mahler and the lengthy tone poems of Richard Strauss such as *Ein Heldenleben* (A Hero's Life) and *Thus Spake Zarathustra.*

In 1914, the English composer Gustav Holst began work on his suite called *The Planets,* for which the following are needed:

4 flutes, alto flute and 2 piccolos	large percussion section including:
4 oboes, bass oboe and 2 cors anglais	6 kettle drums
3 clarinets and bass clarinet	bass drum
3 bassoons and double bassoon	snare drum
6 horns	cymbals
4 trumpets	triangle
3 trombones	tambourine
tenor and bass tubas	glockenspiel
	xylophone
organ	celesta
	tubular bells
	tam-tam
very large string section including 2 harps	also, in the final piece: choir of female voices

But at the same time, from about 1910 onwards, some composers (either by choice or from financial pressures – an orchestra as huge as that shown above is costly to employ!) went to the opposite extreme and began to write for much smaller orchestras consisting of a small body of strings, one or two each of various kinds of woodwind and brass, and perhaps one or two players controlling a varied selection of percussion instruments. Other composers have experimented with new sounds and new techniques, making use of newly invented instruments, discovering interesting new sounds from familiar instruments and, more recently, exploring the exciting possibilities of electronic sounds – perhaps creating a tape of these sounds to be played back through loud-speakers in the concert hall and blended with the sounds of the orchestra, as in Roberto Gerhard's Symphony No. 3 ('Collages'); or actually using electronic equipment in the concert hall to alter and transform the sounds of the orchestral instruments in various ways, as in Stockhausen's *Mixtur,* composed in 1964. A performance of *Mixtur* needs:

five orchestral groups:	1	*pizzicato* strings (including harp)
	2	bowed strings
	3	woodwind
	4	brass
	5	percussion
four sine wave generators		
four ring modulators		

The percussion group is separately amplified. Sounds from the other four orchestral groups are fed by microphones, together with electronic sounds from the four sine wave modulators, into the four ring modulators. (A ring modulator takes any two sounds and by adding their frequencies together produces a third, higher, sound. At the same time, it produces a fourth, lower, sound which represents the difference between their frequencies.)

In *Mixtur,* the 'live' sounds of the orchestral instruments, the sounds of the sine wave generators, and the electronic transformations produced by the ring modulators, result in a rich, fascinating *mixture,* bringing together the familiar – and the unfamiliar.

Music to hear for full orchestra

A   Listen to the final Fugue from Benjamin Britten's *The Young Person's Guide to the Orchestra.* One instrument plays the fugue-tune on its own, then another kind of instrument joins in which the same tune, then a third, and so on – until all the instruments of Britten's orchestra have played the tune in turn.

Here is the fugue-tune:

(piccolo)   (flute enters)

And this is the order in which the instruments are heard:

woodwind: piccolo, flutes, oboes, clarinets, bassoons

strings: first violins, second violins, violas, cellos, double basses, harp

brass: horns, trumpets, trombones and tuba

percussion (playing together): xylophone, kettle drums, bass drum, snare drum, cymbals, tambourine, tam-tam

At the end, Purcell's theme (on which Britten has based his Variations) returns slowly and majestically on the brass, while the rest of the orchestra continues to play Britten's fugue-tune.

B Here are a few more, out of a great many, pieces which demonstrate a large orchestra used in a particularly colourful or interesting way:

Berlioz: 'March to the Scaffold', and 'Dream of a Witches' Sabbath' from *Symphonie Fantastique*
Wagner: 'The Ride of the Valkyries'; 'Siegfried's Funeral March'
Tchaikovsky: third movement from Symphony No. 6 ('Pathétique')
Rimsky-Korsakov: *Spanish Caprice*
Copland: *Rodeo; Appalachian Spring*
Concertos for Orchestra by Bartók, Tippett, Lutosławski

Assignment 28

Of the pieces mentioned in this chapter which you have listened to, in which do you find the orchestra presents:
(a) the most *balanced* sounds?
(b) the most *interesting* sounds?

Give reasons to support your choices.

Project file

Describe some of the ways in which the orchestra has changed over the past four centuries, mentioning the order in which the four orchestral sections became established.